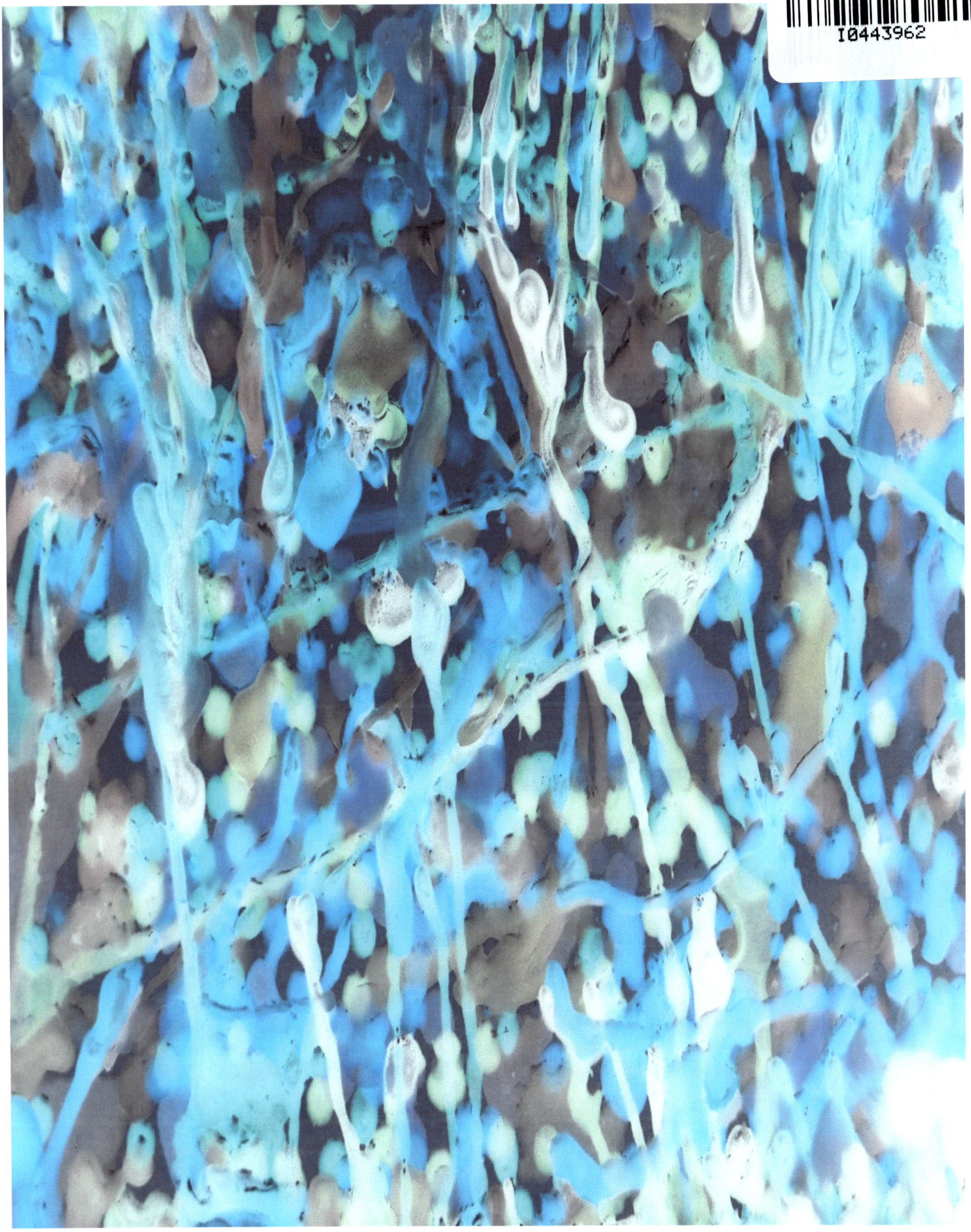

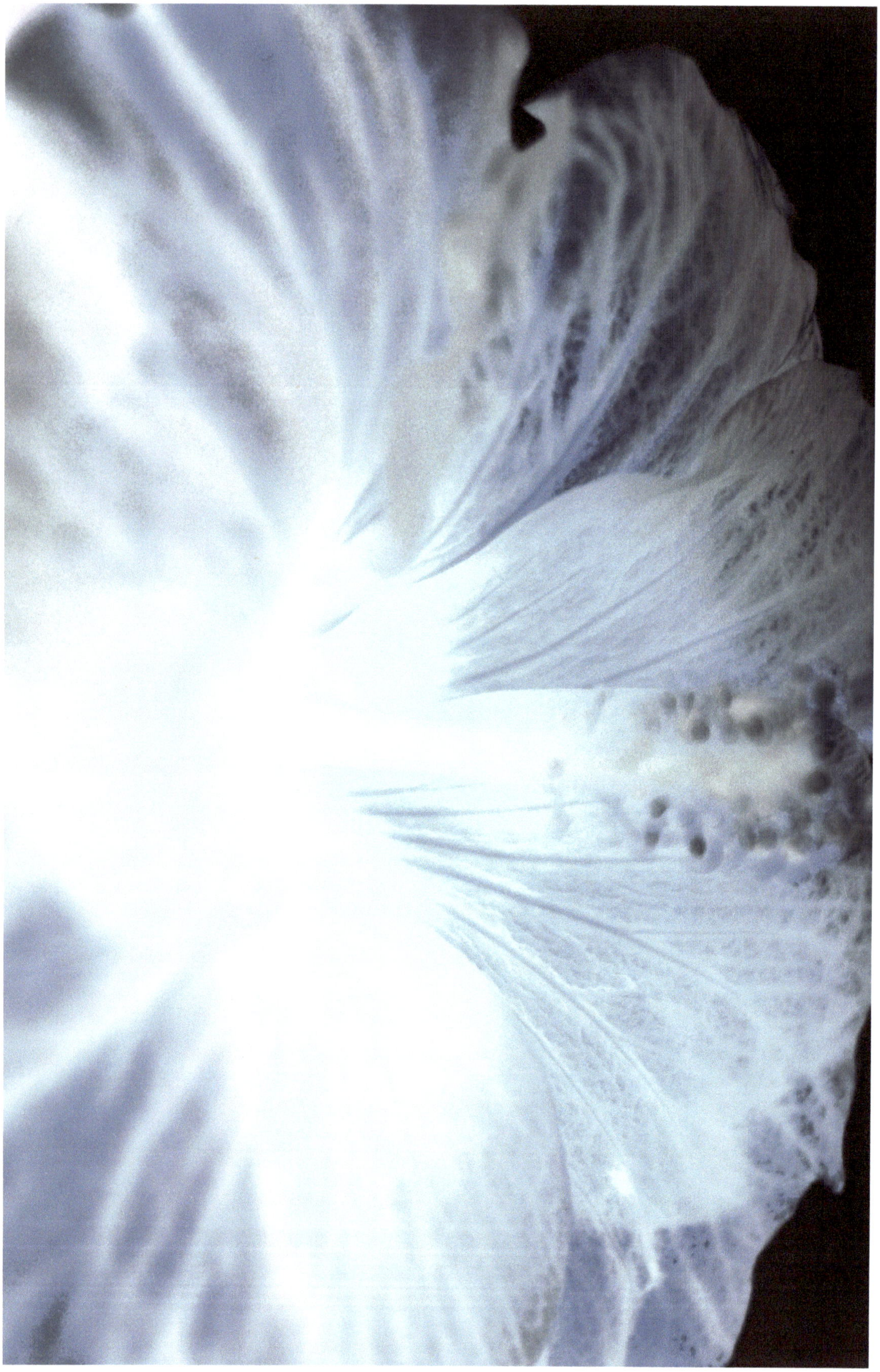

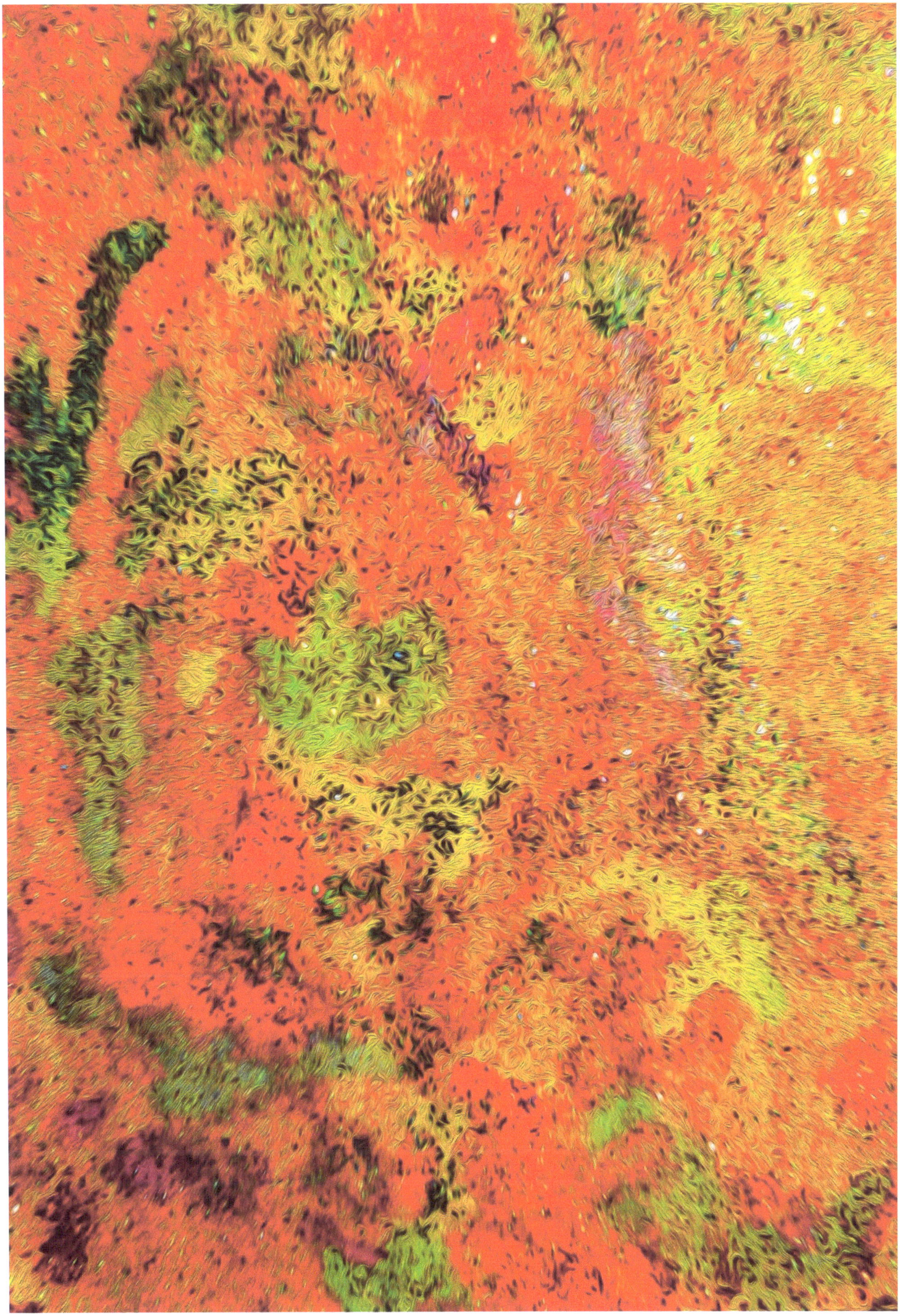

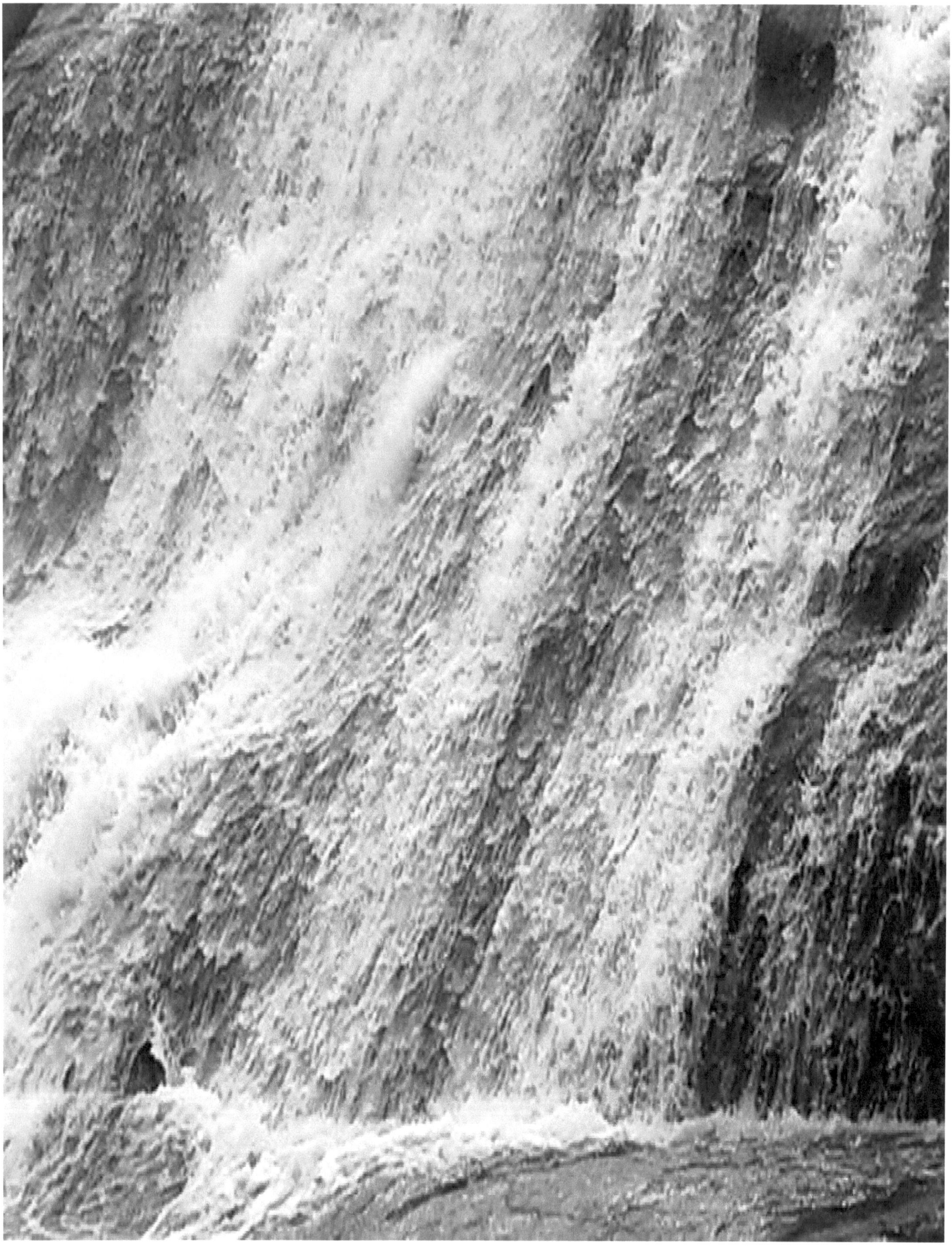

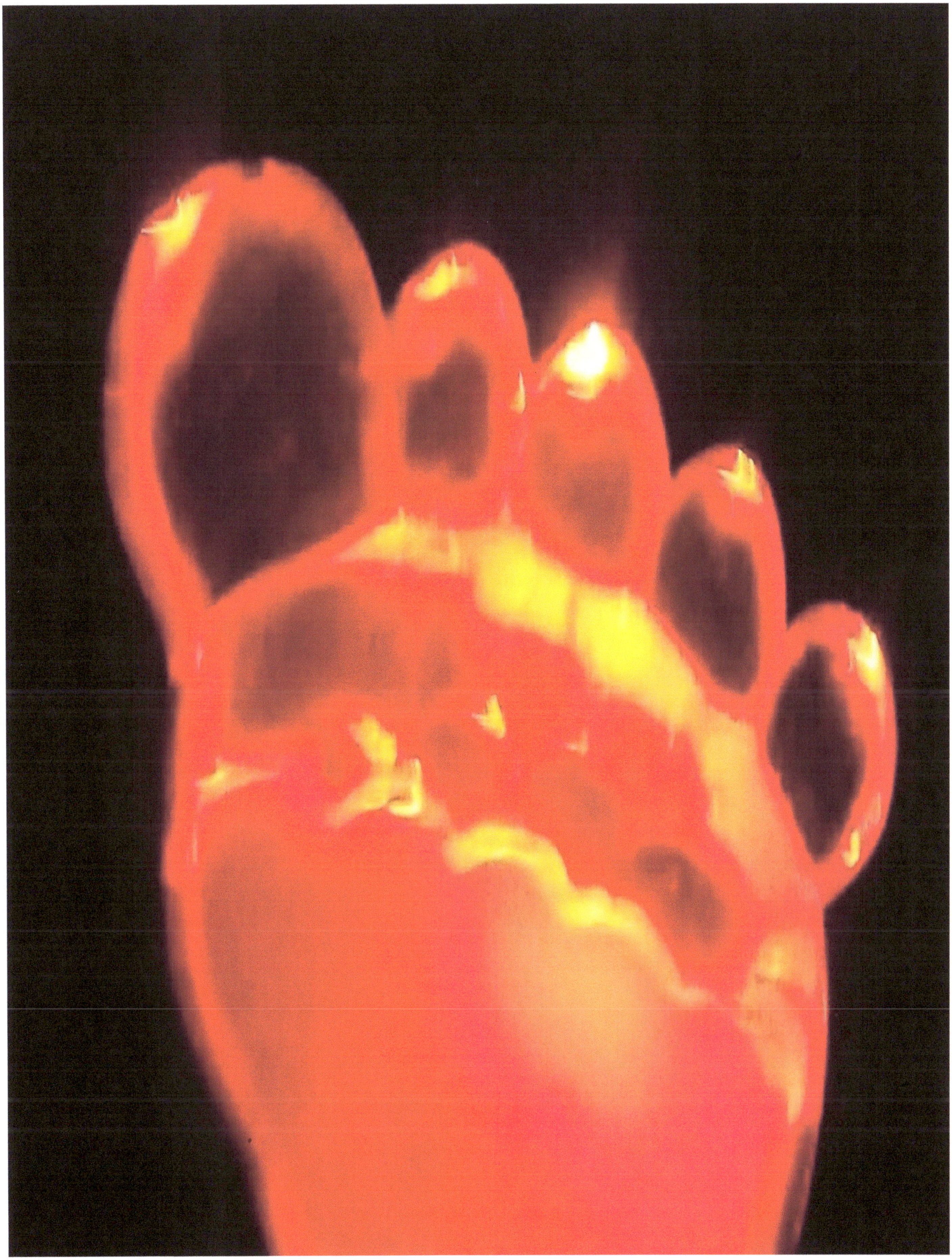

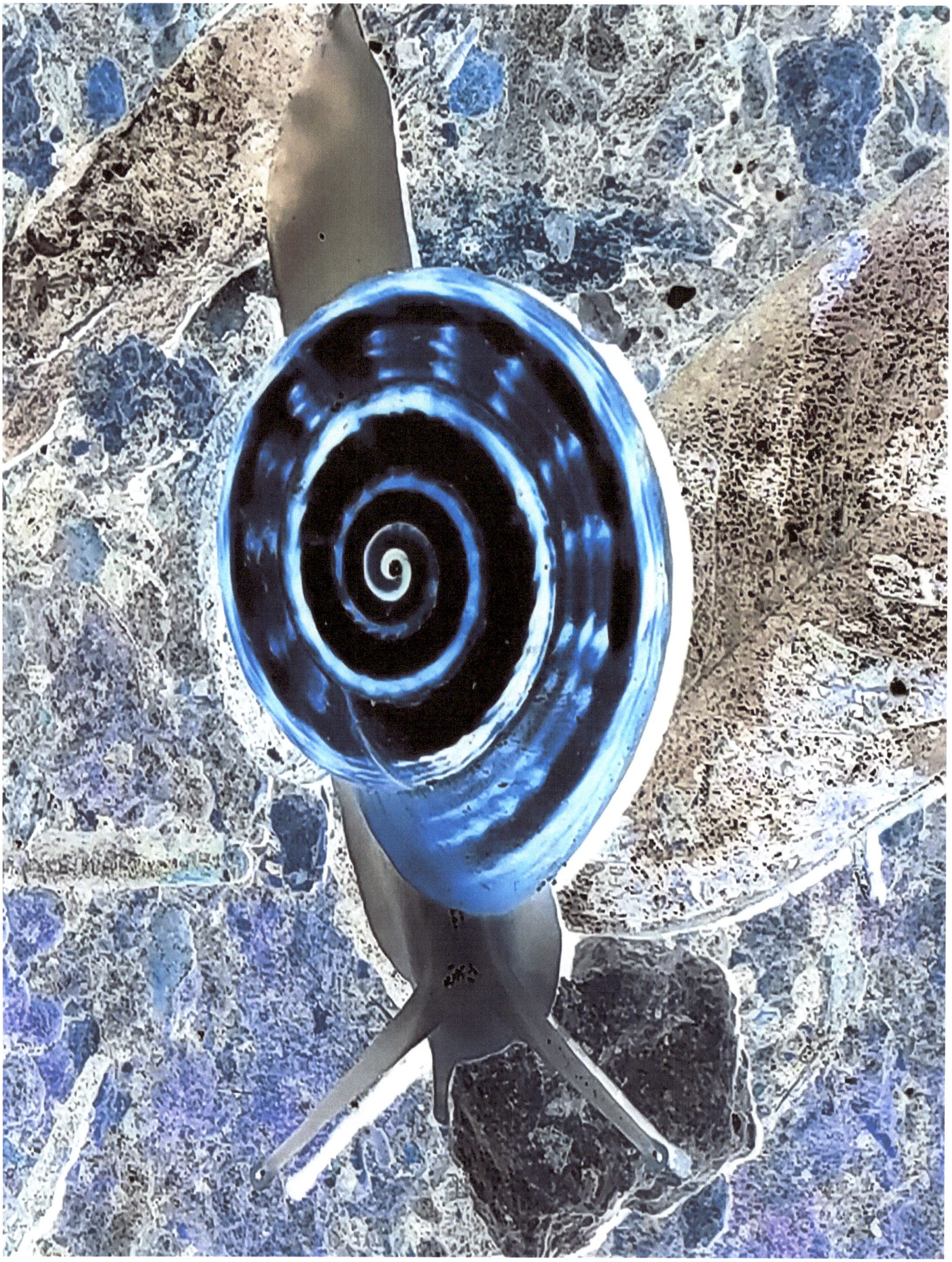

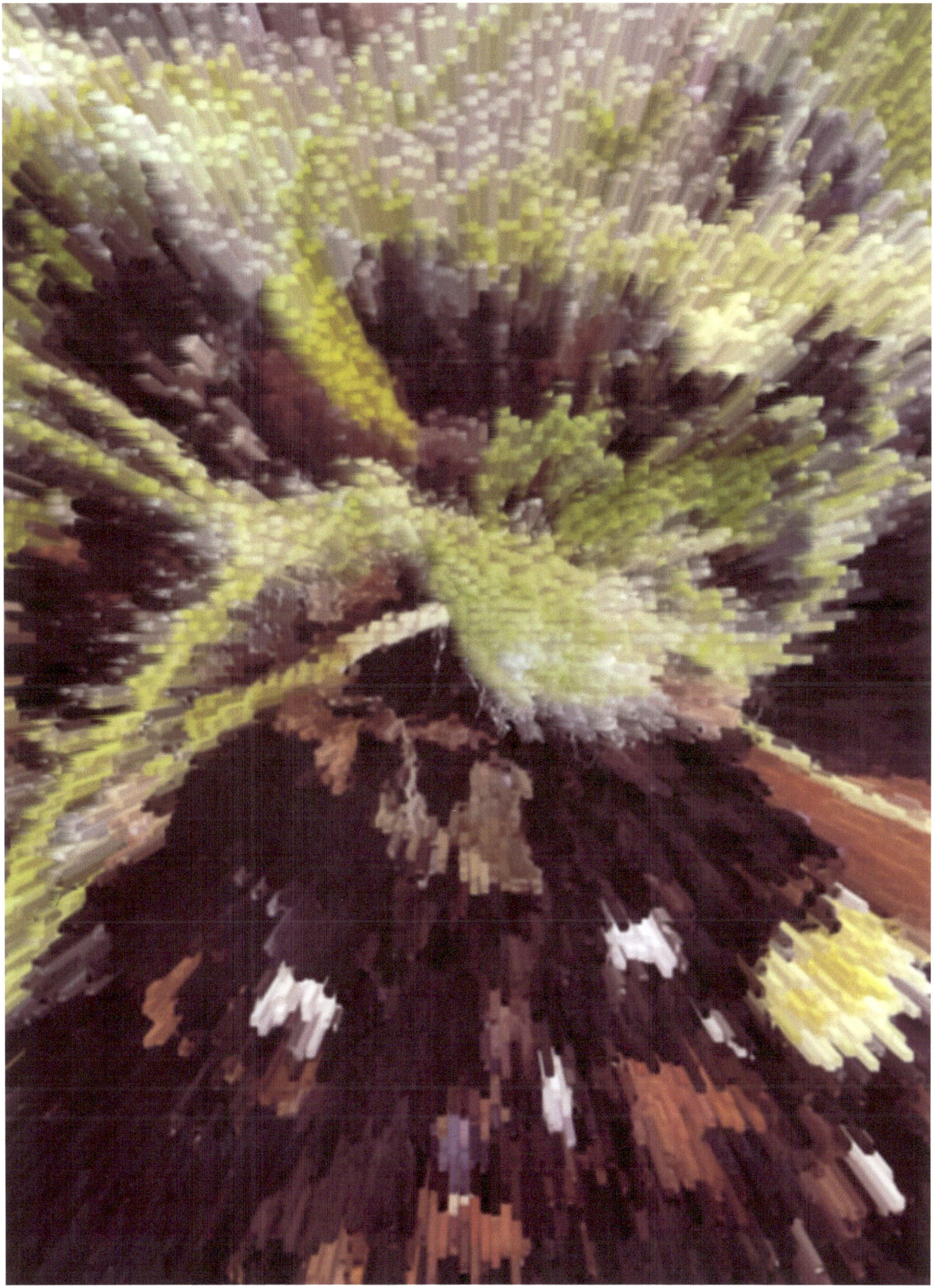

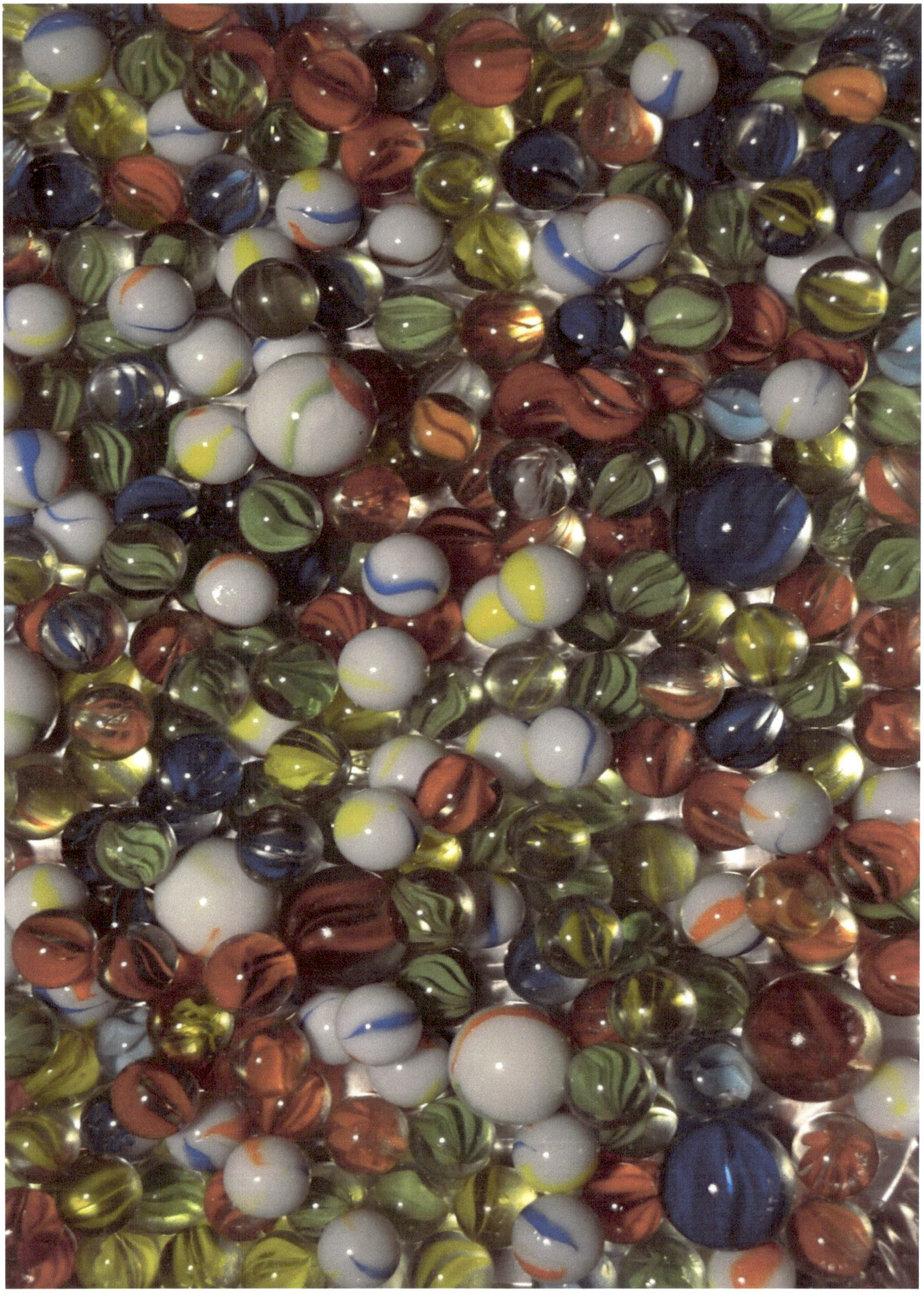

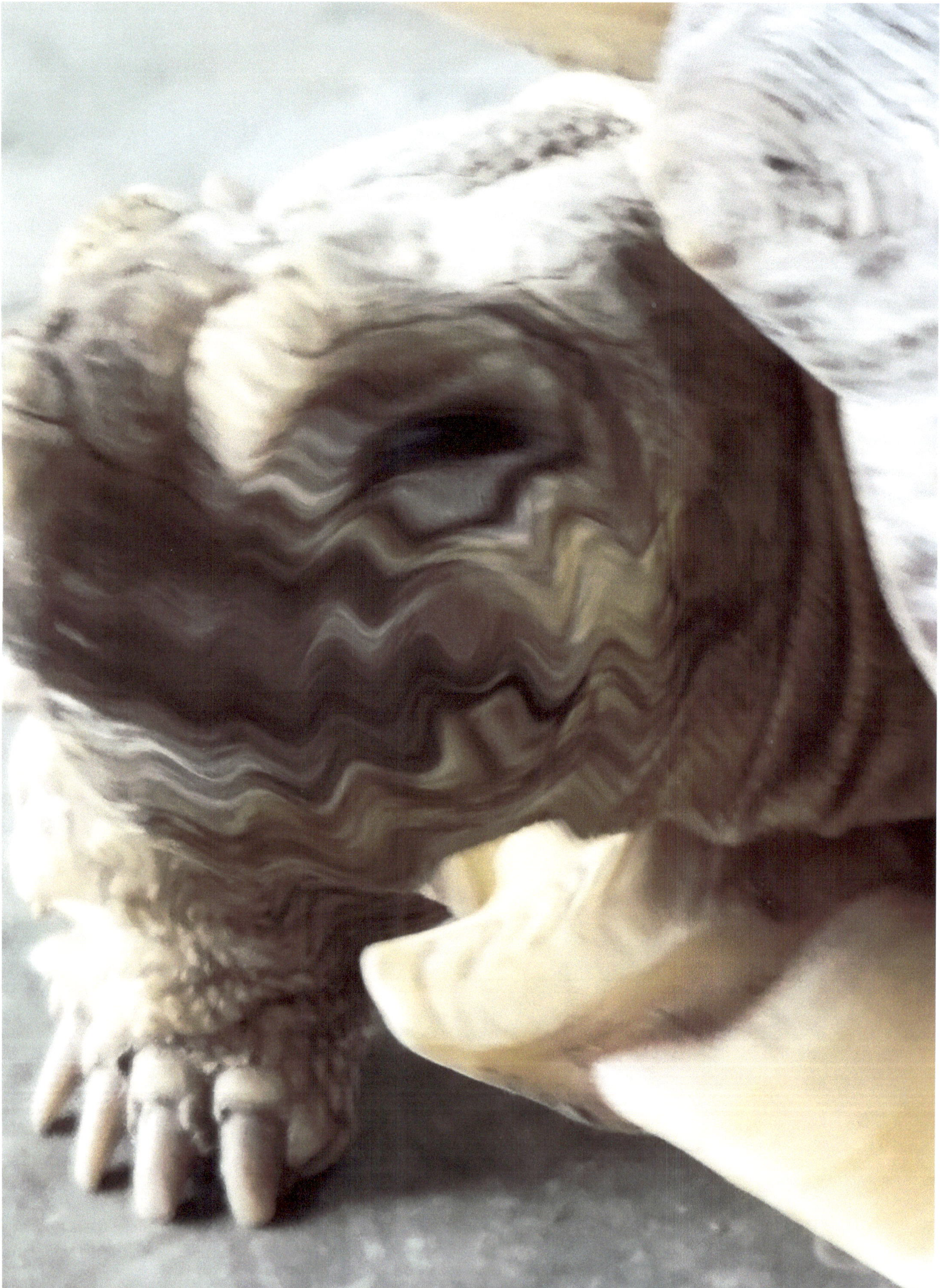

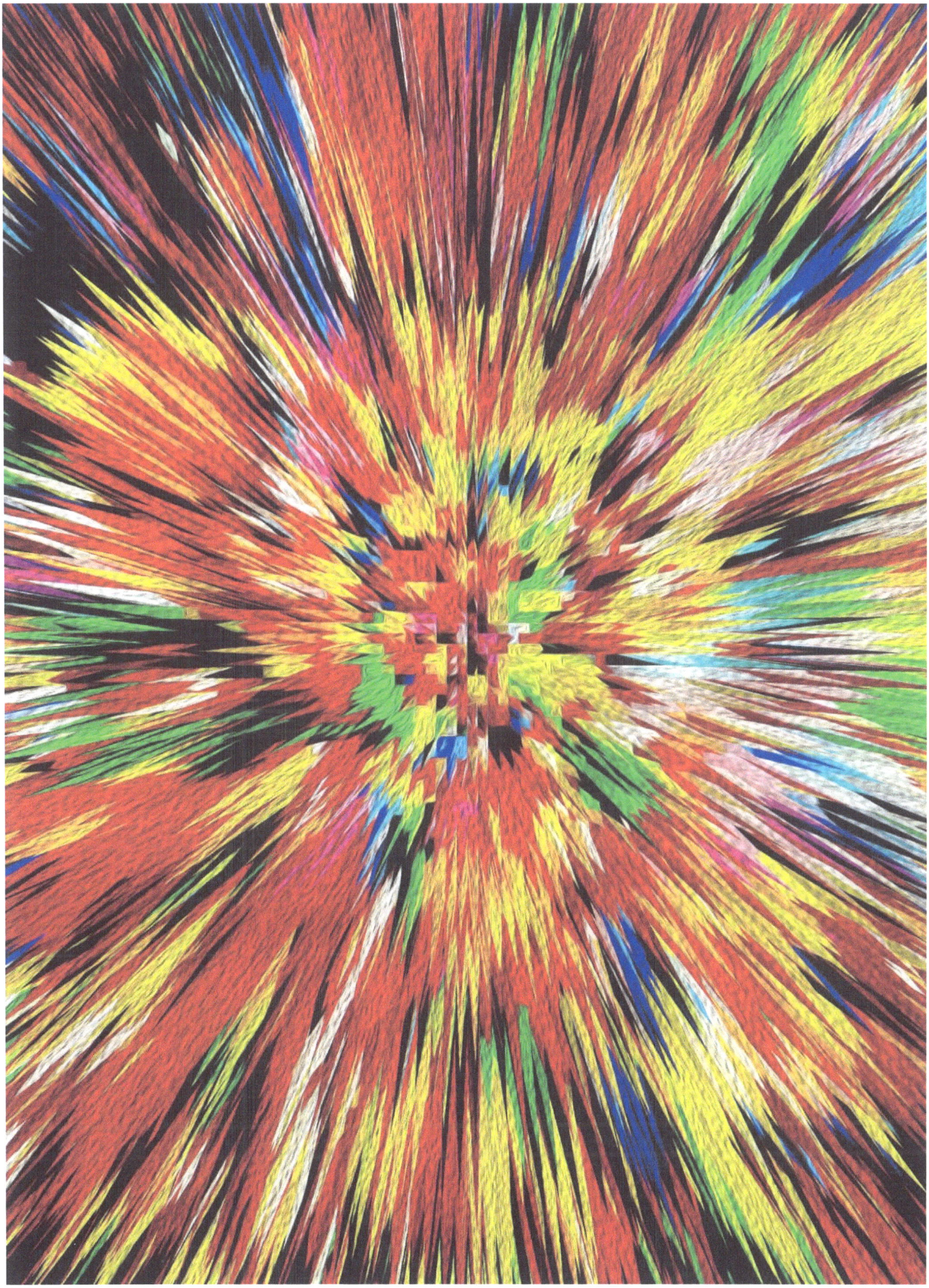

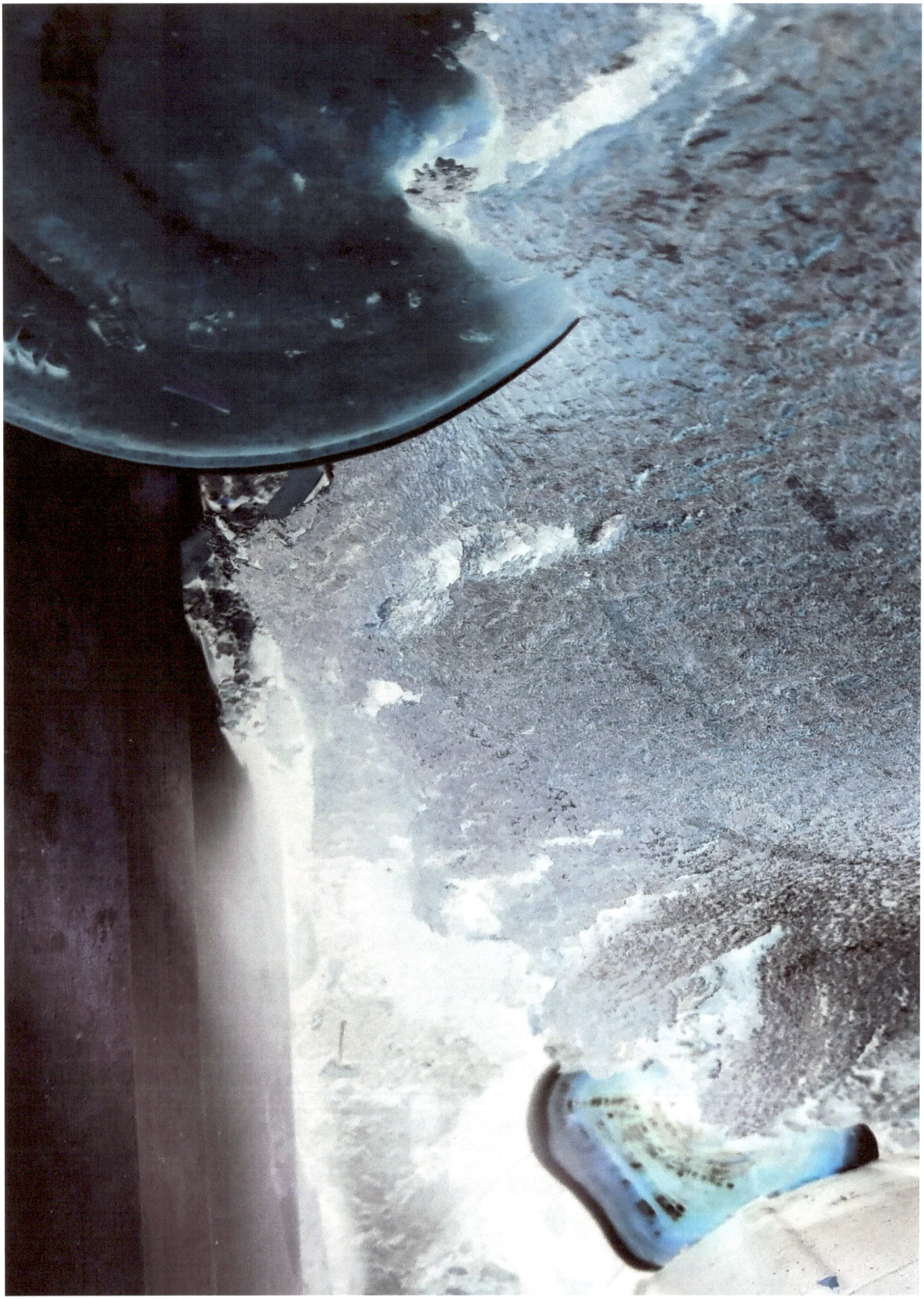

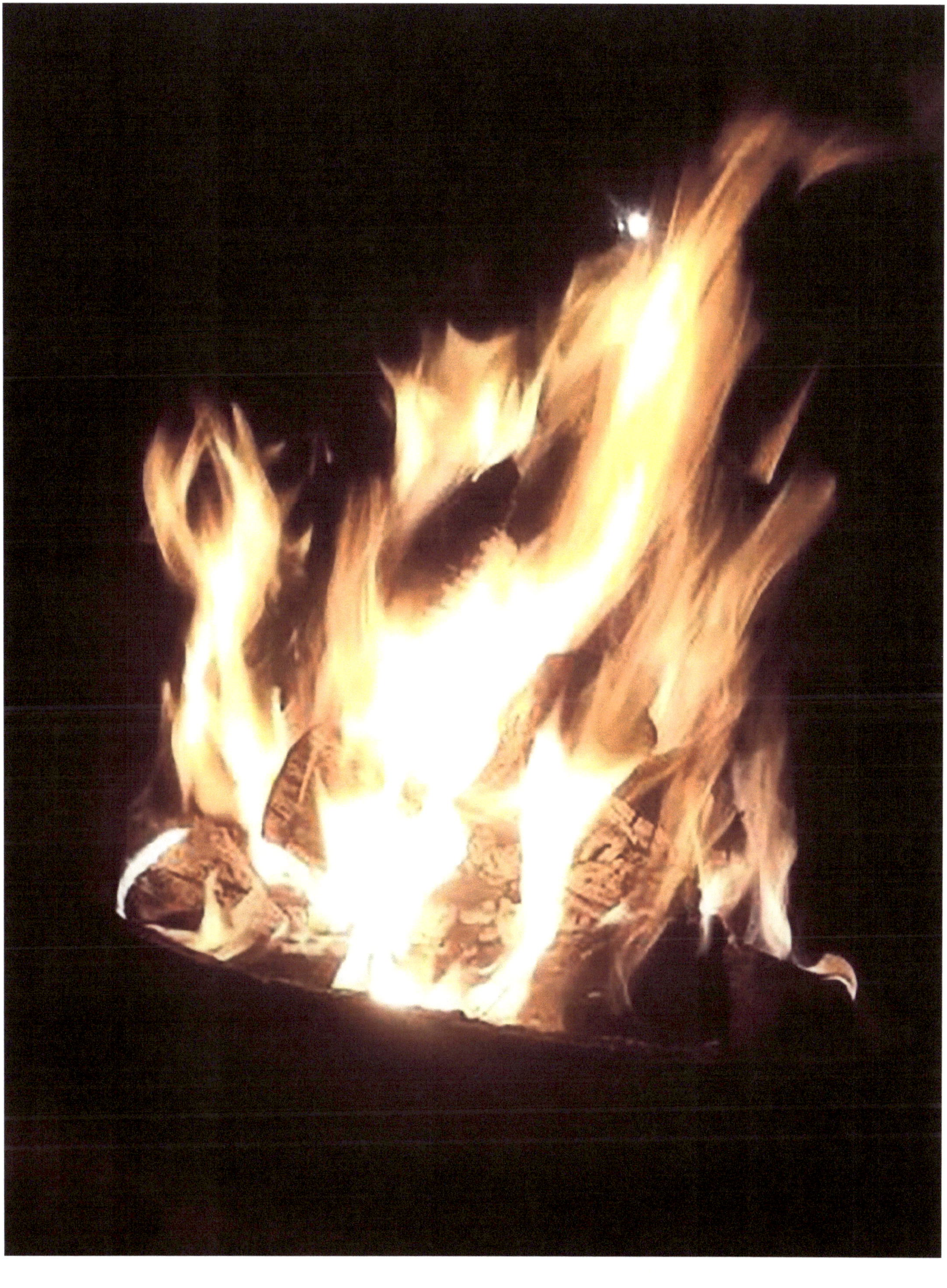

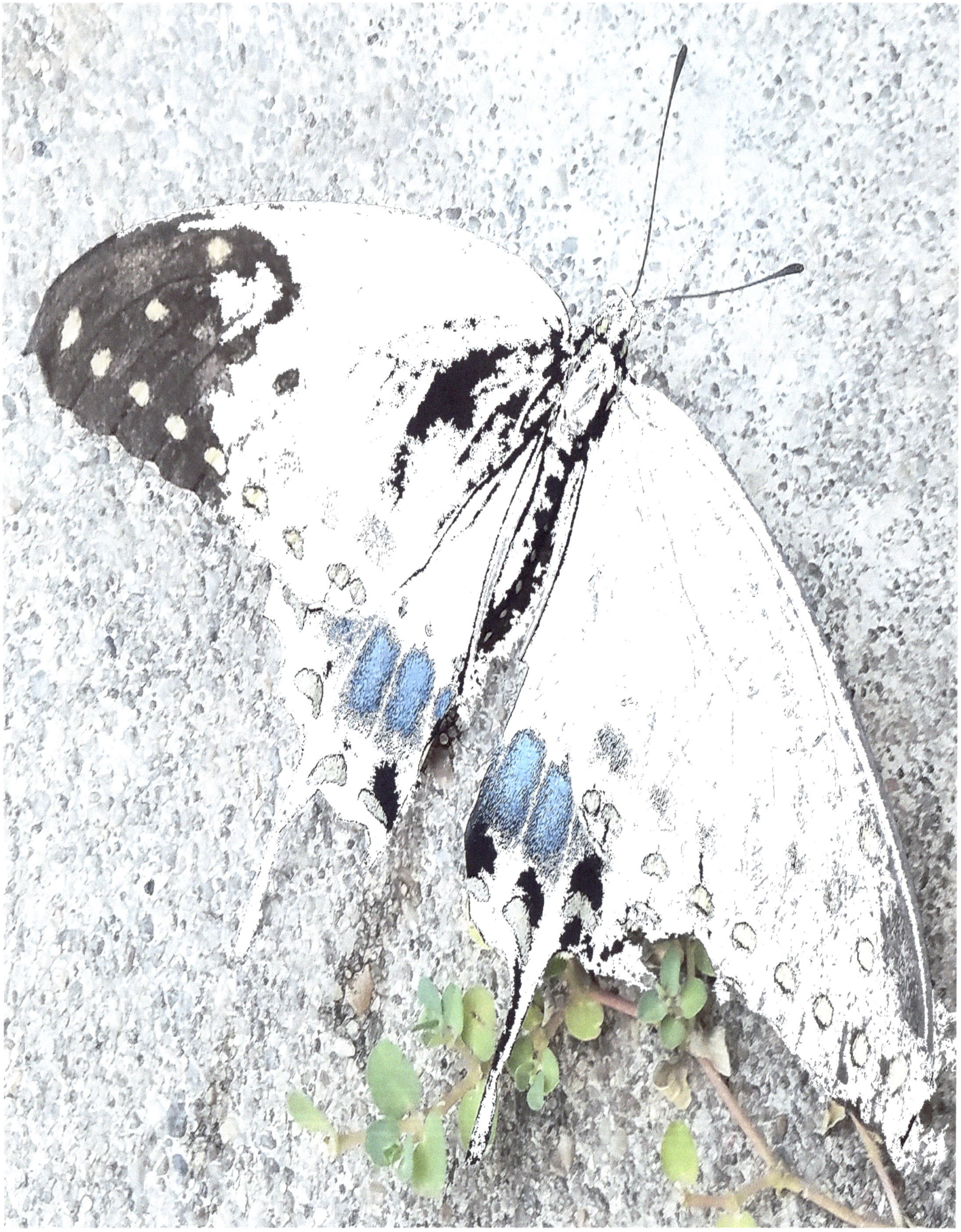

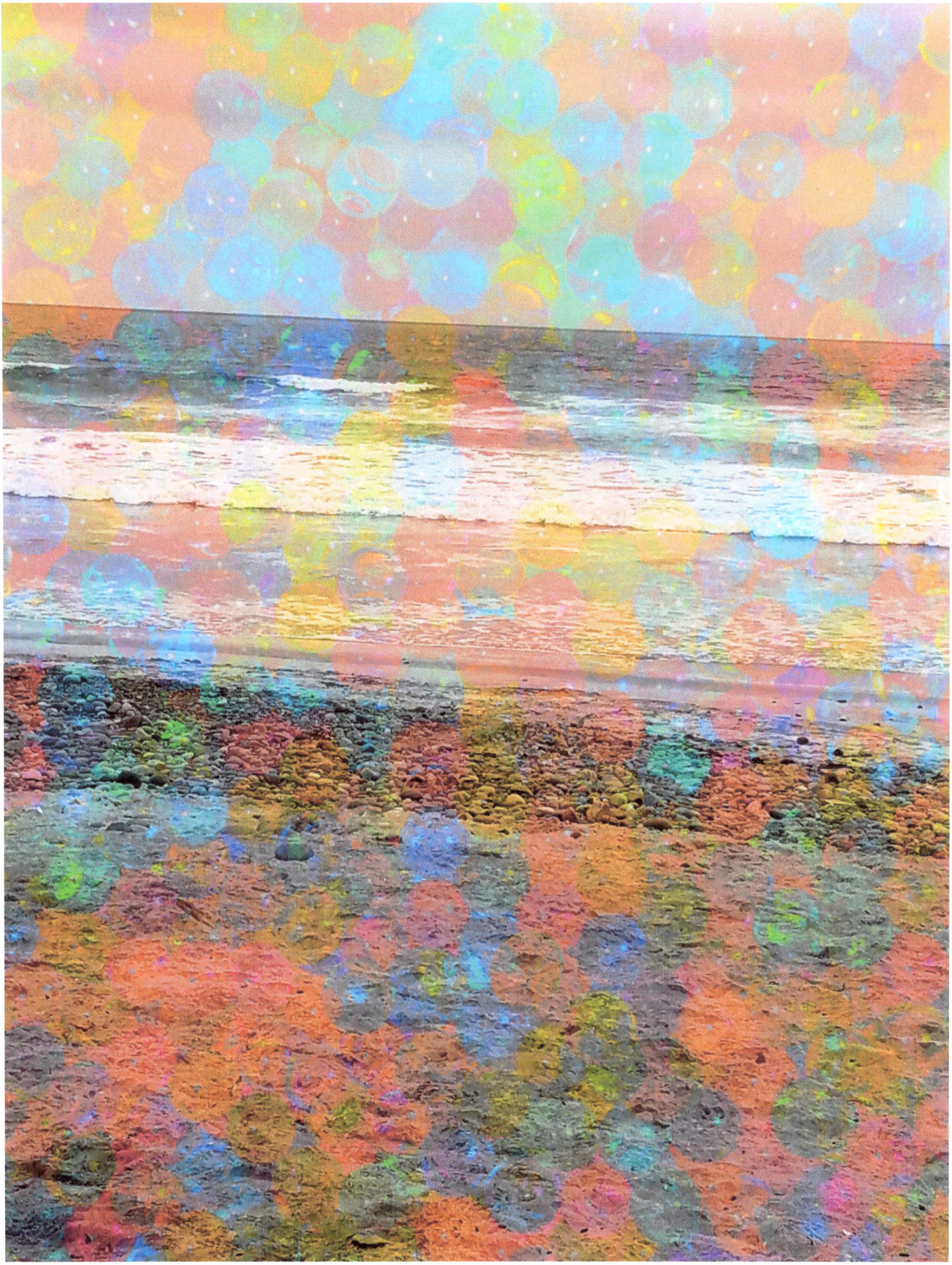

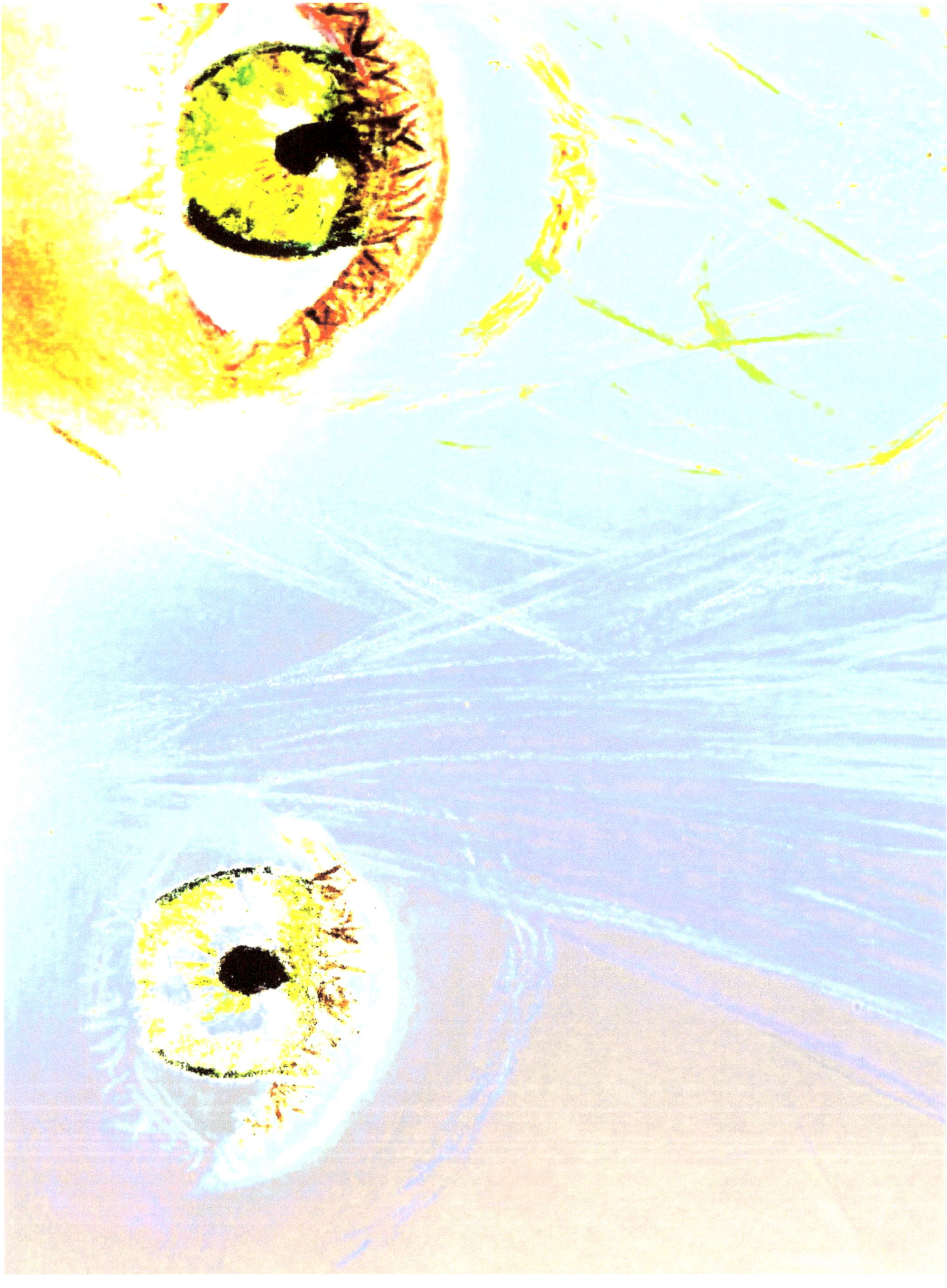

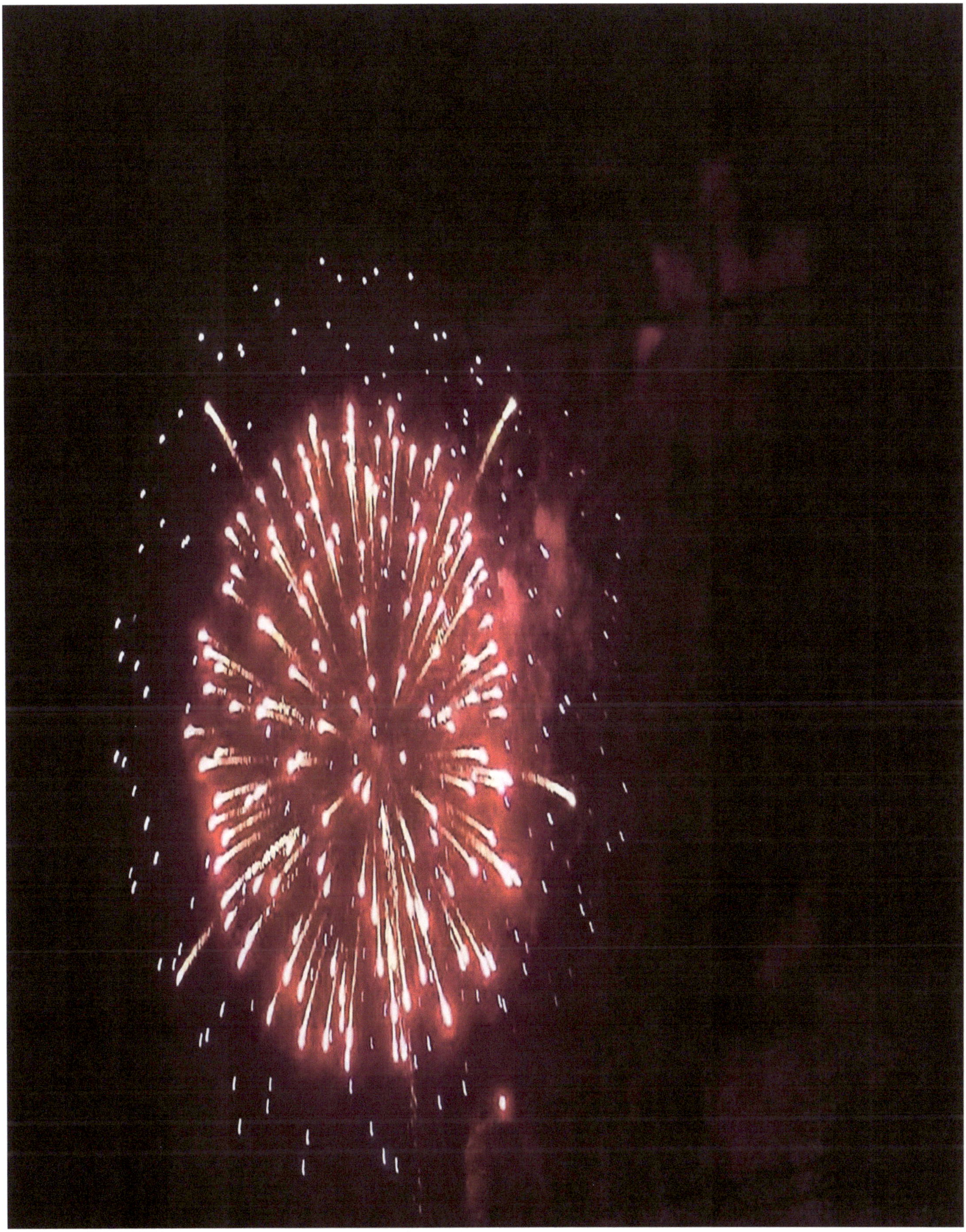

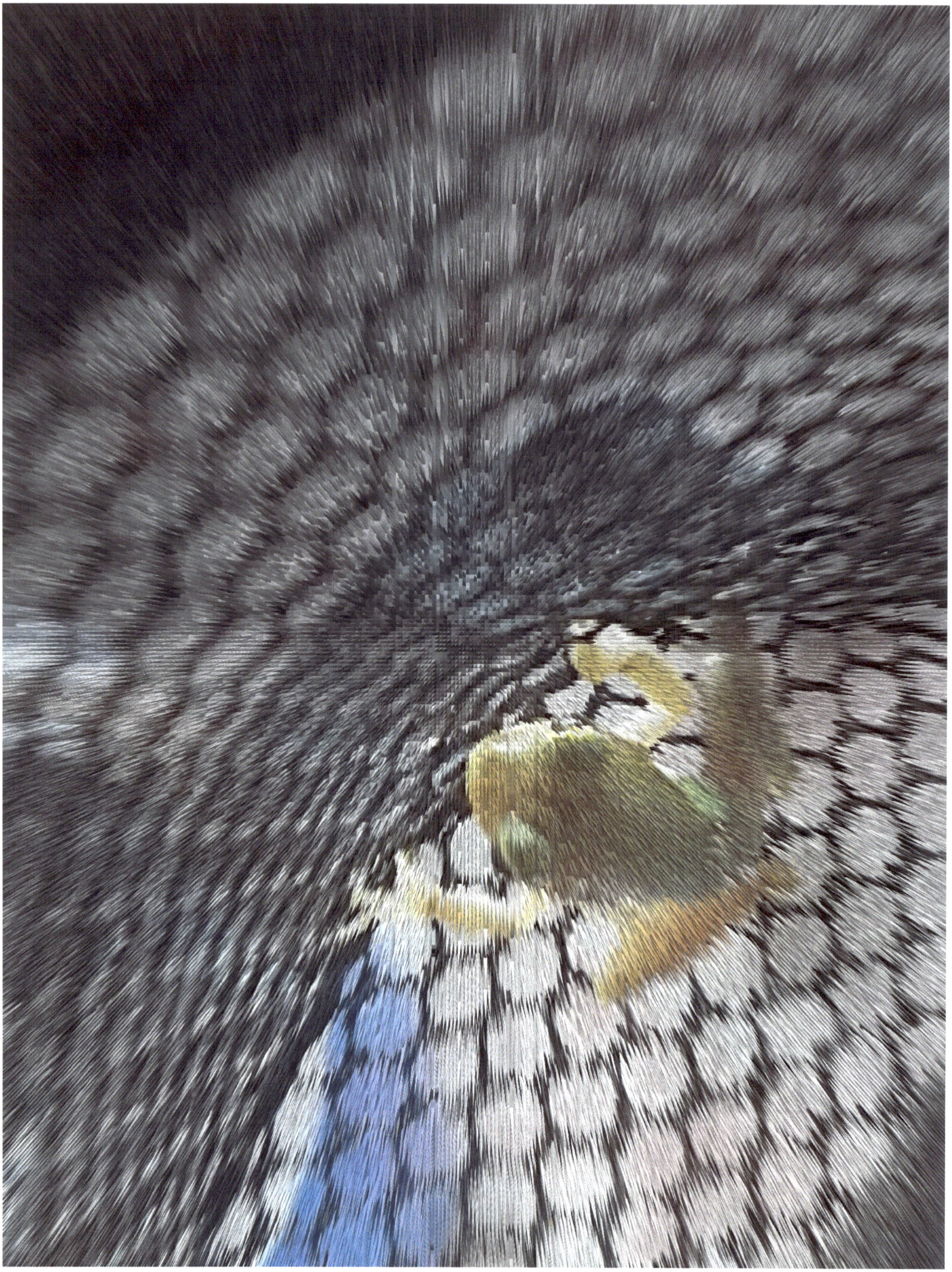

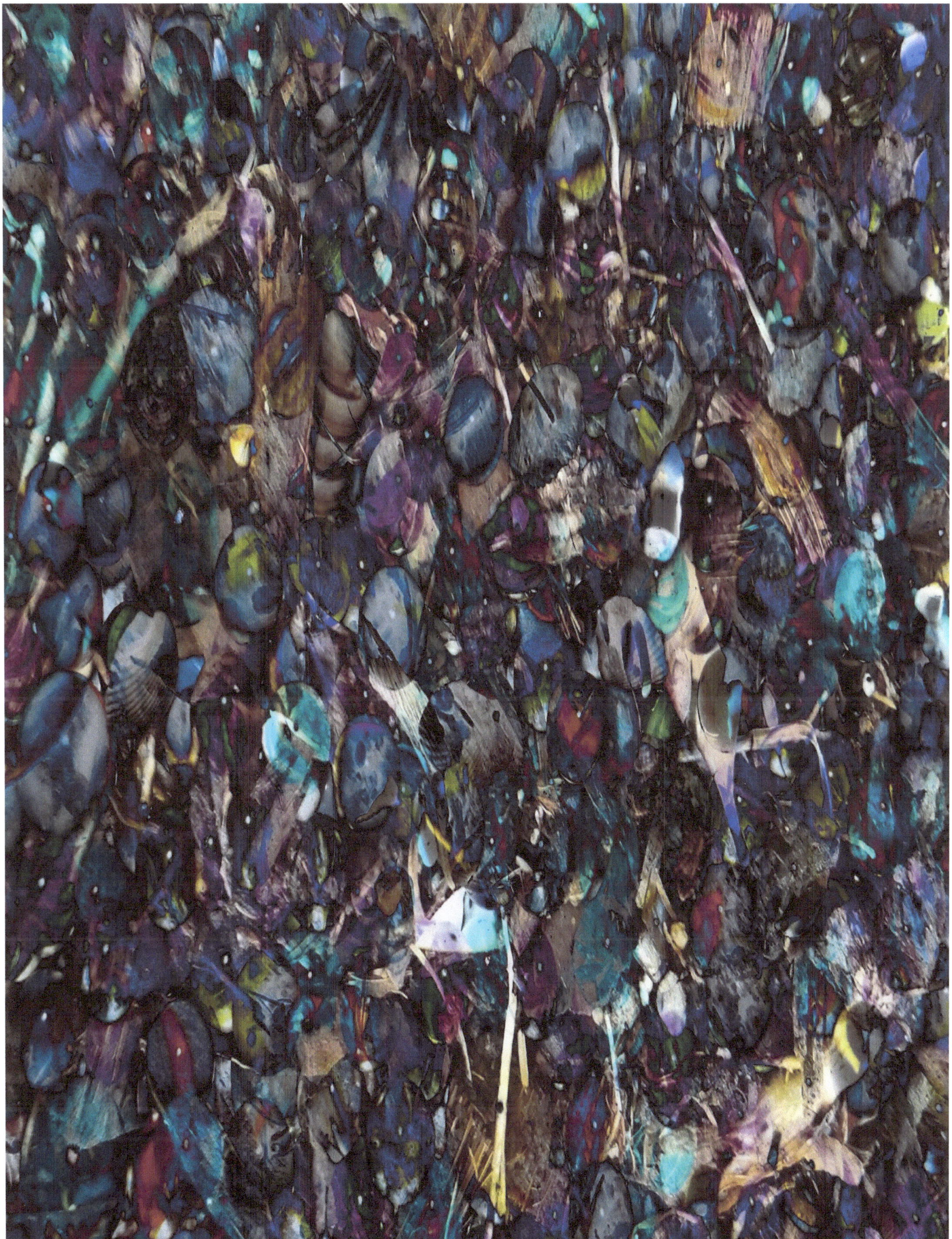

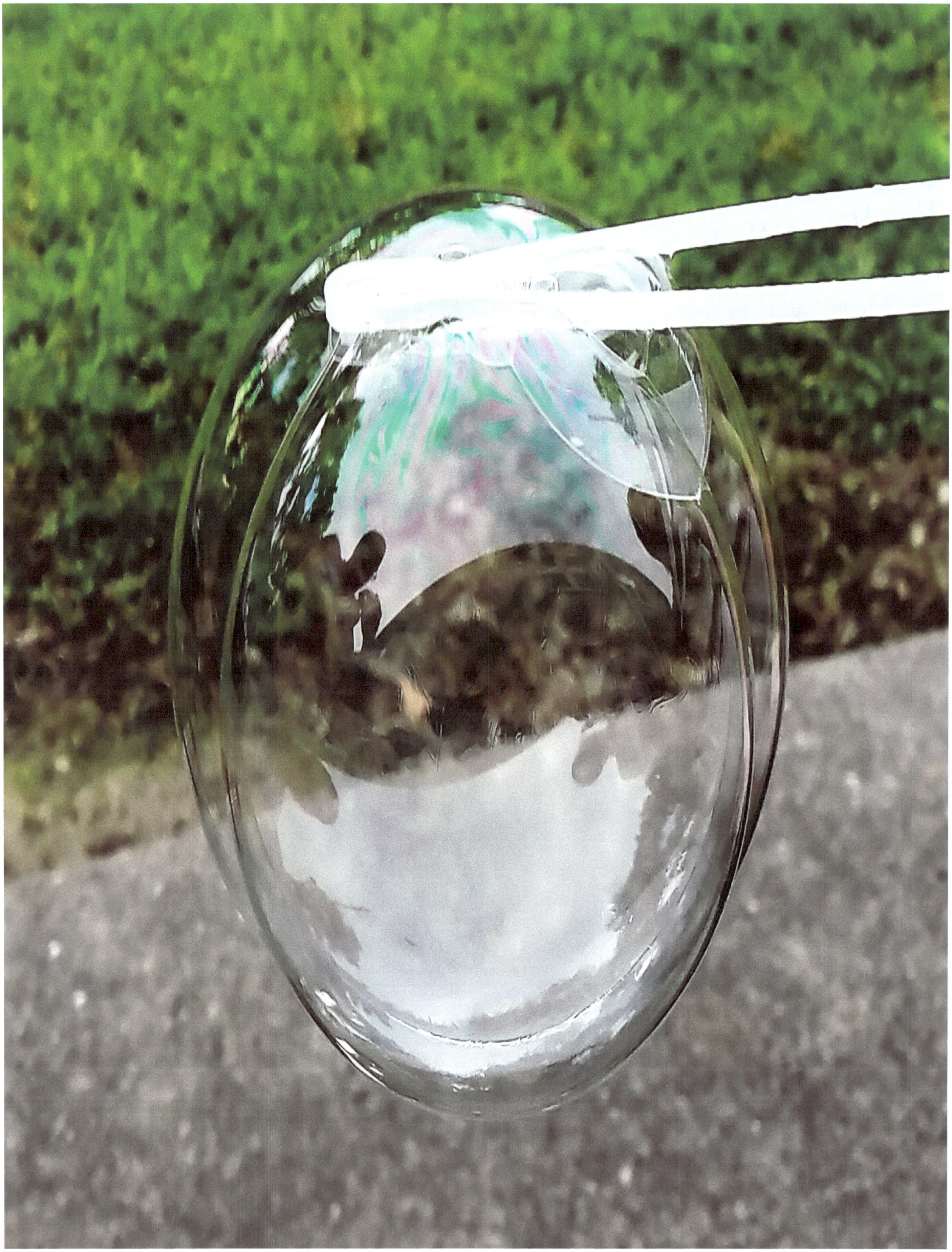

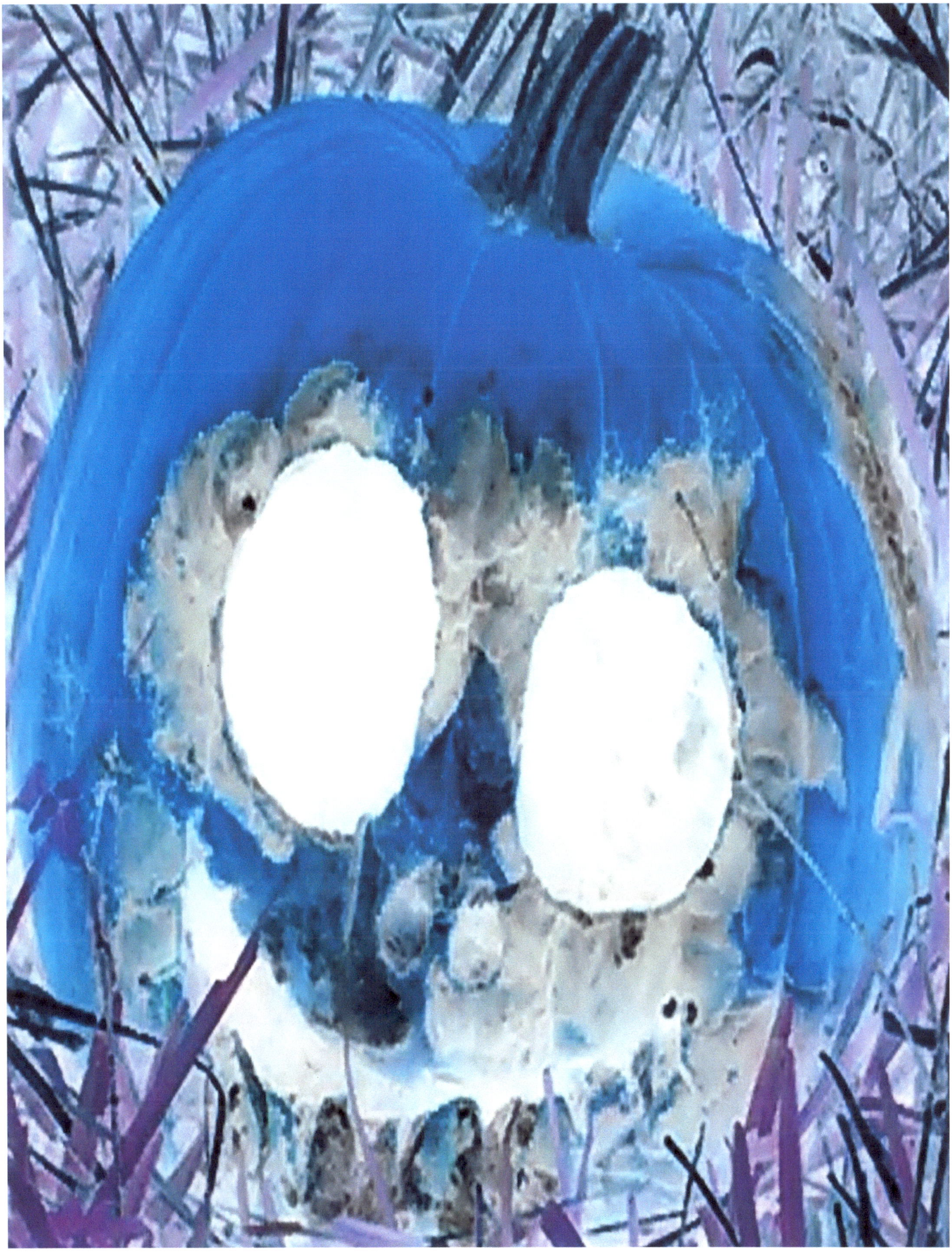

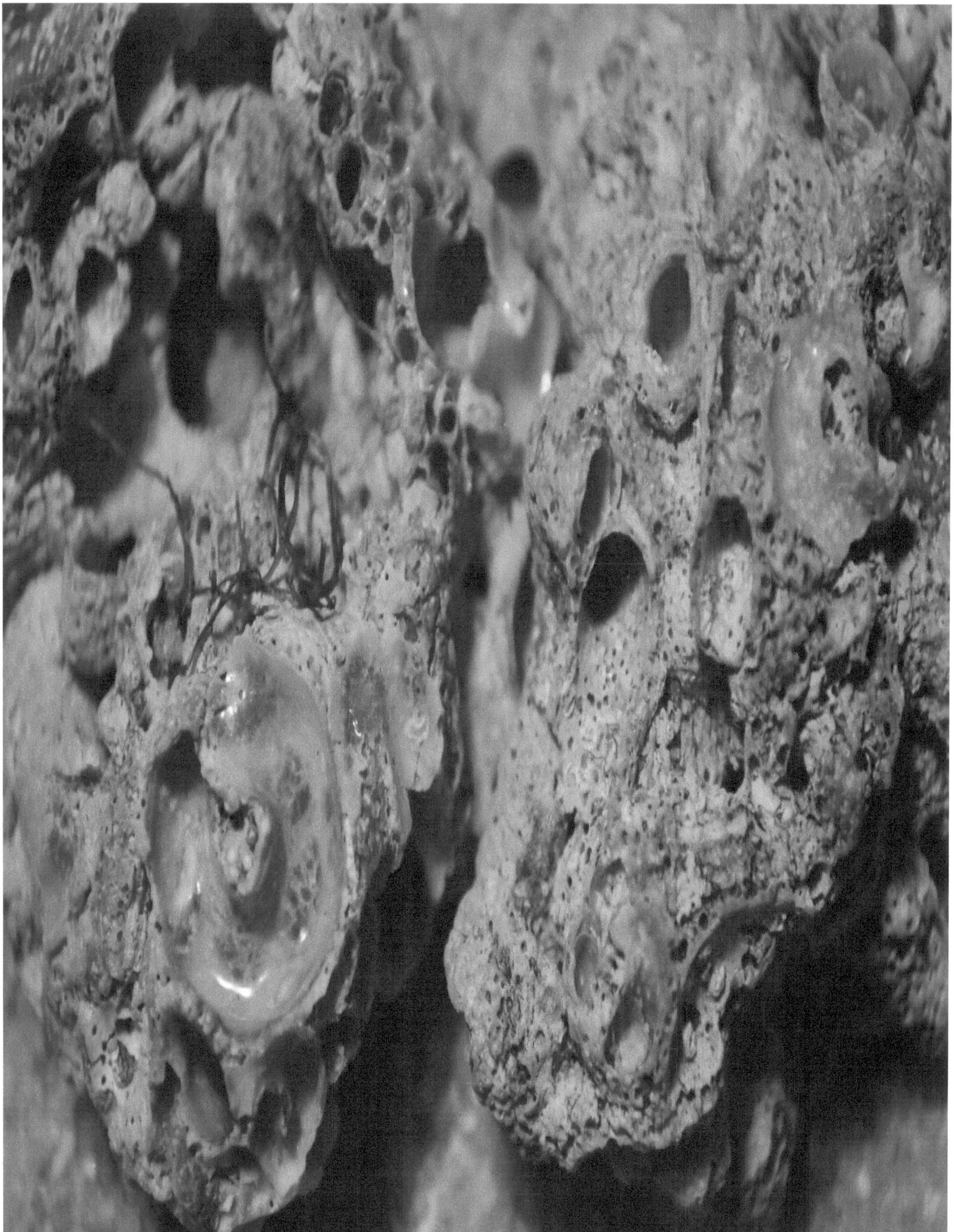

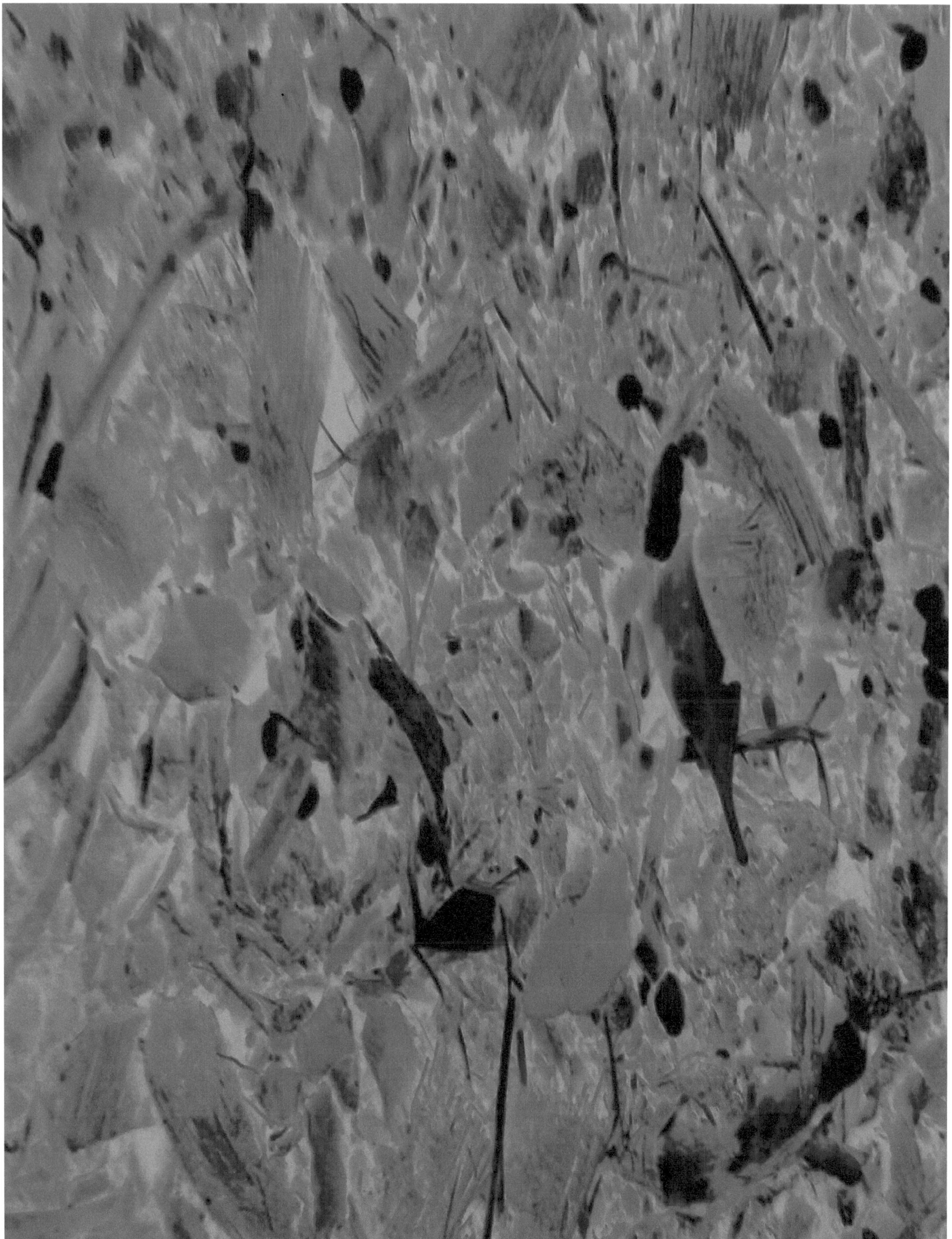

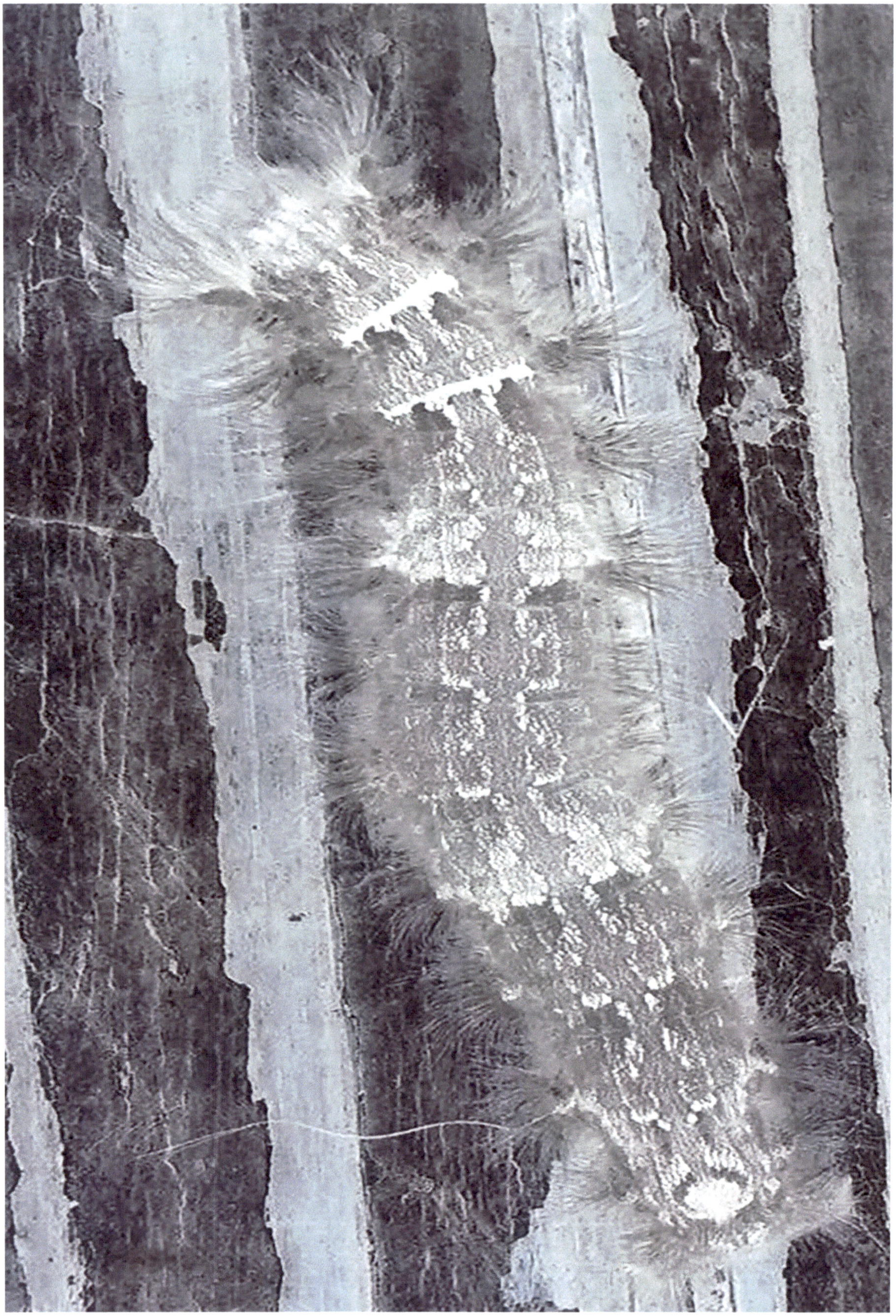

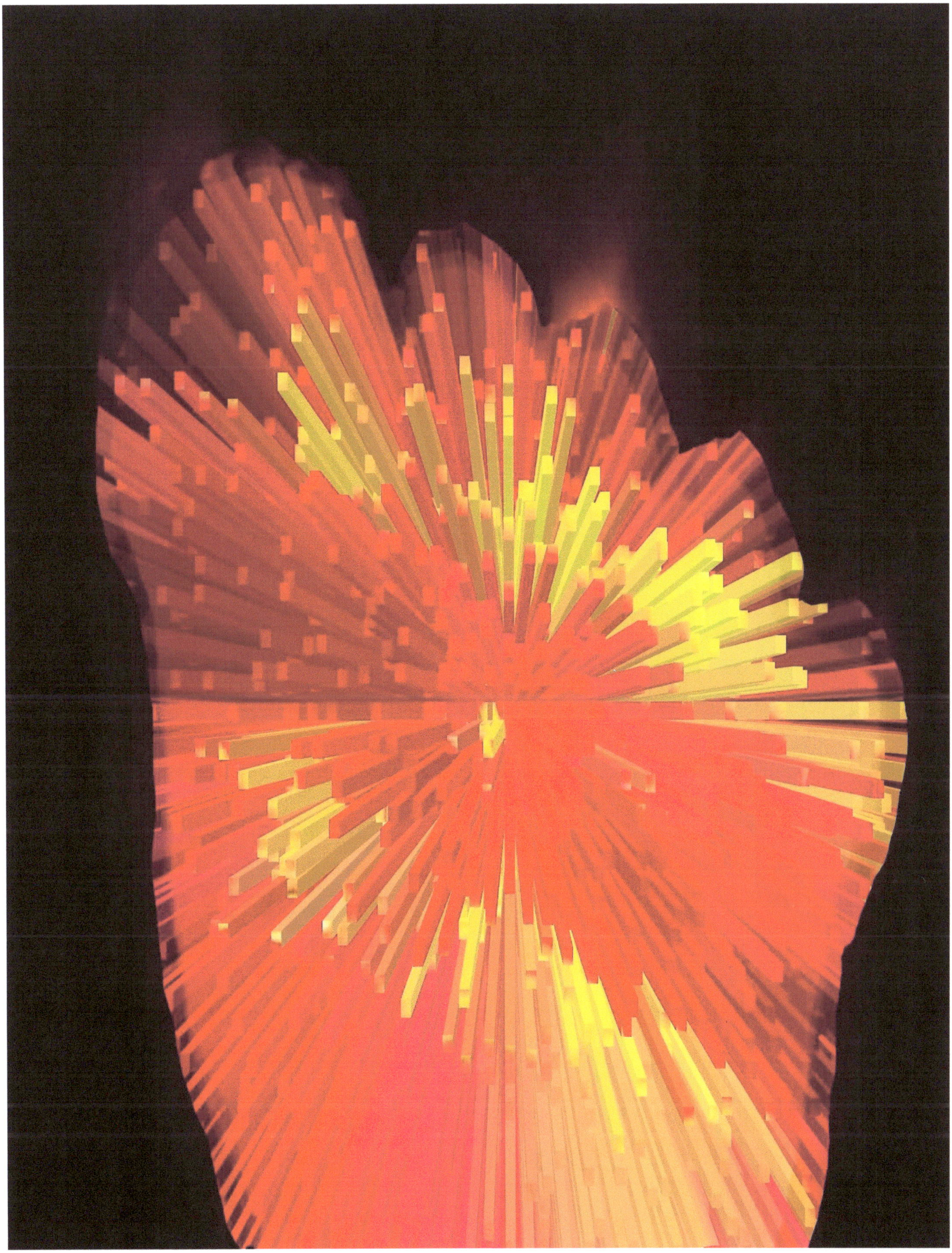

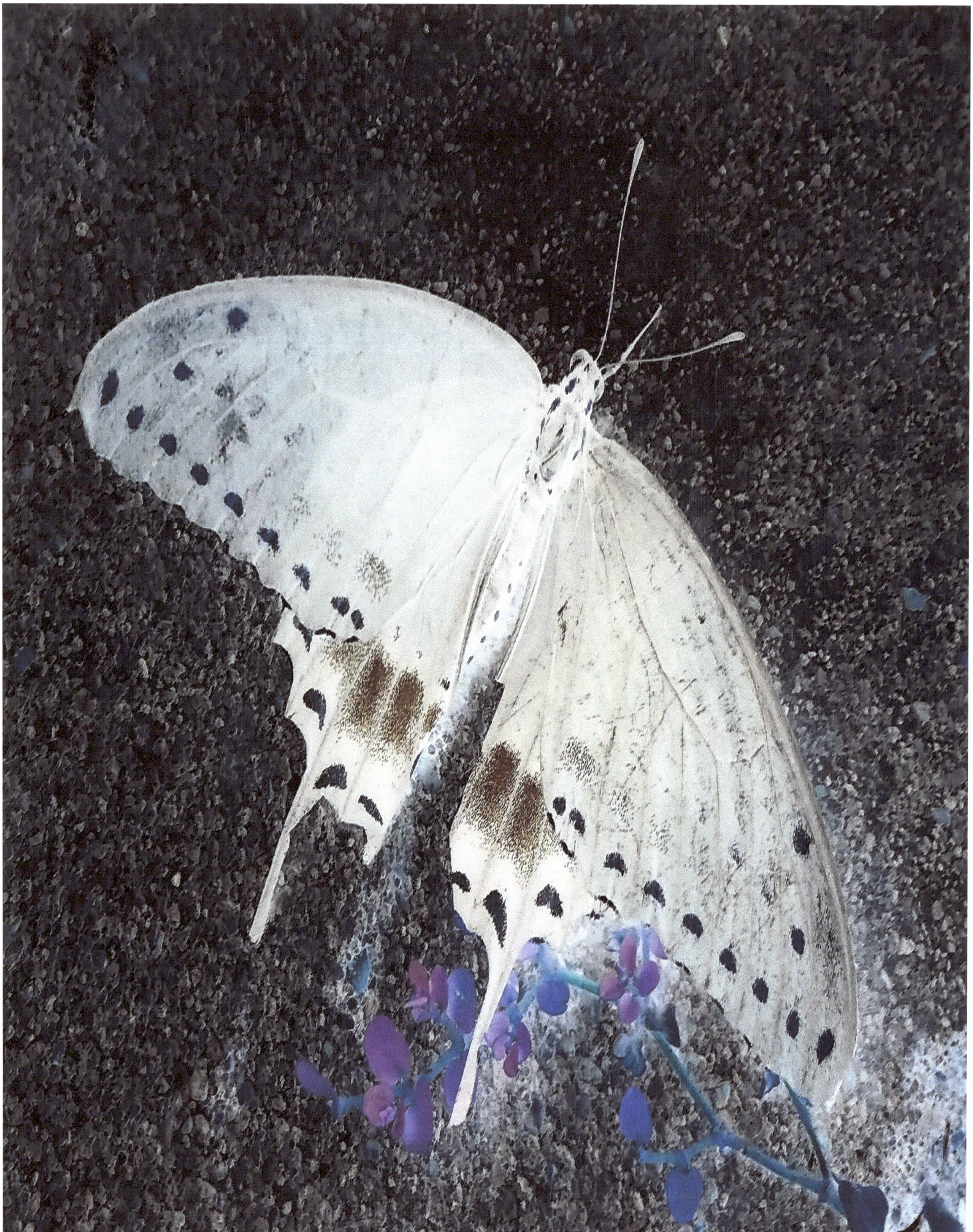

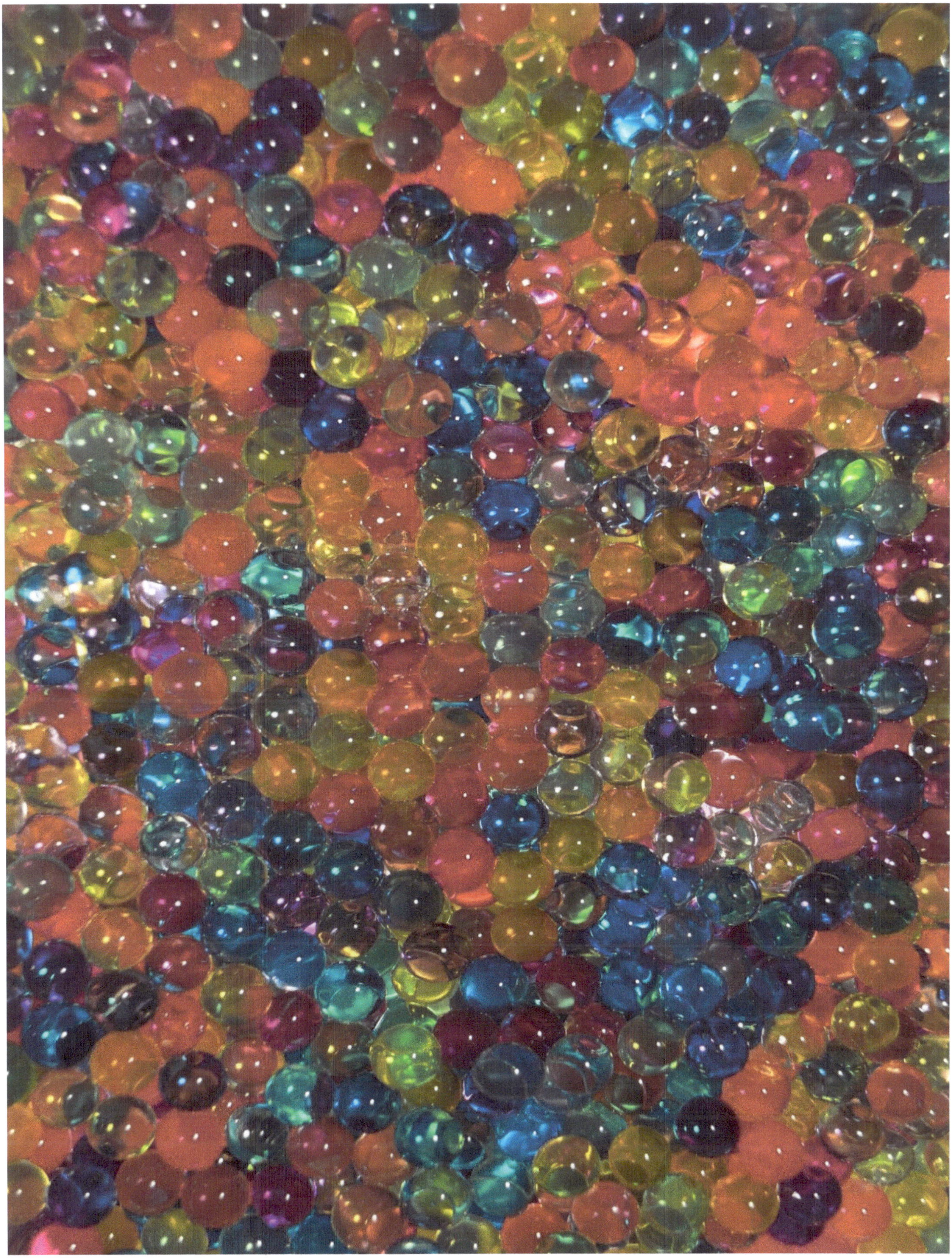

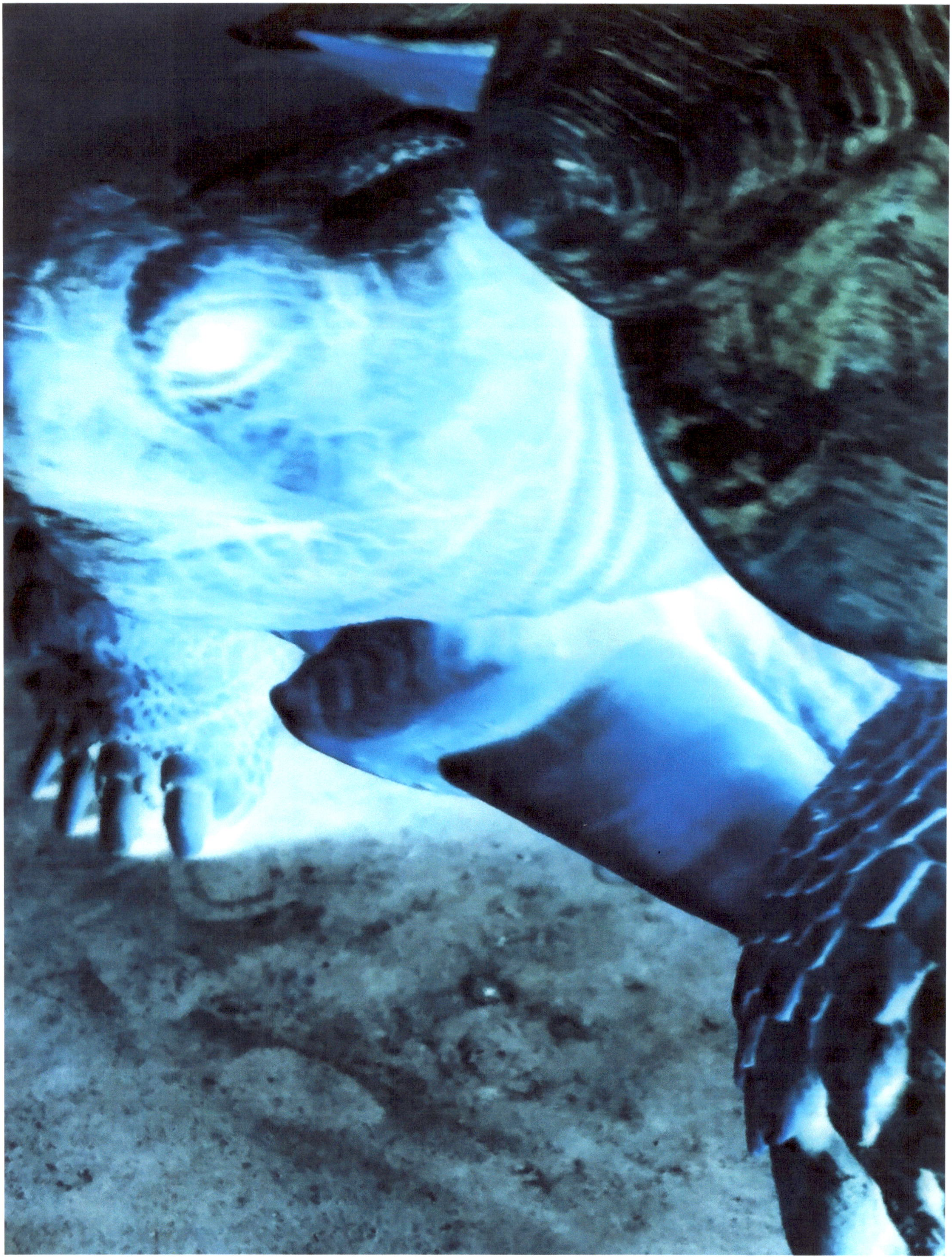

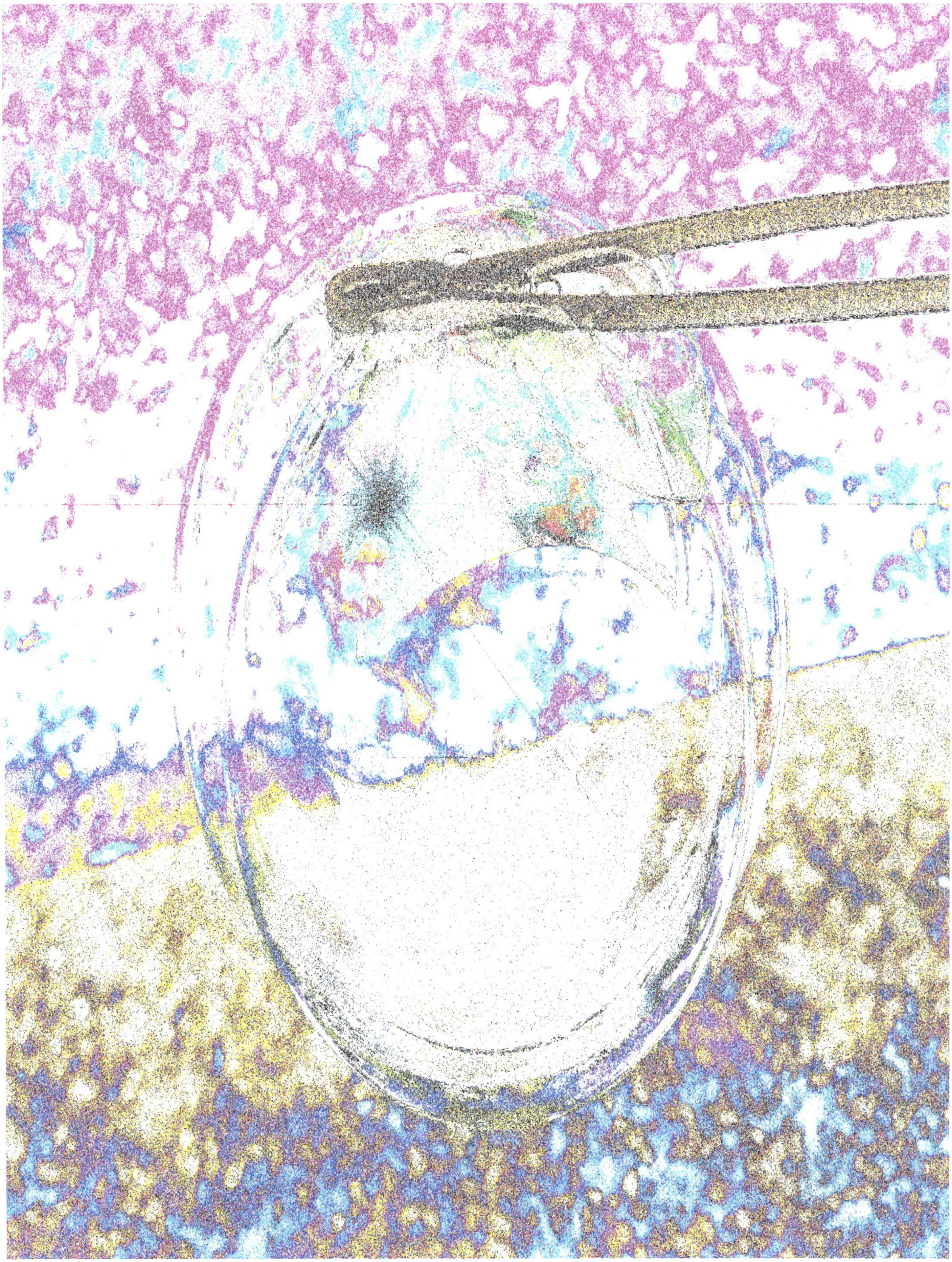

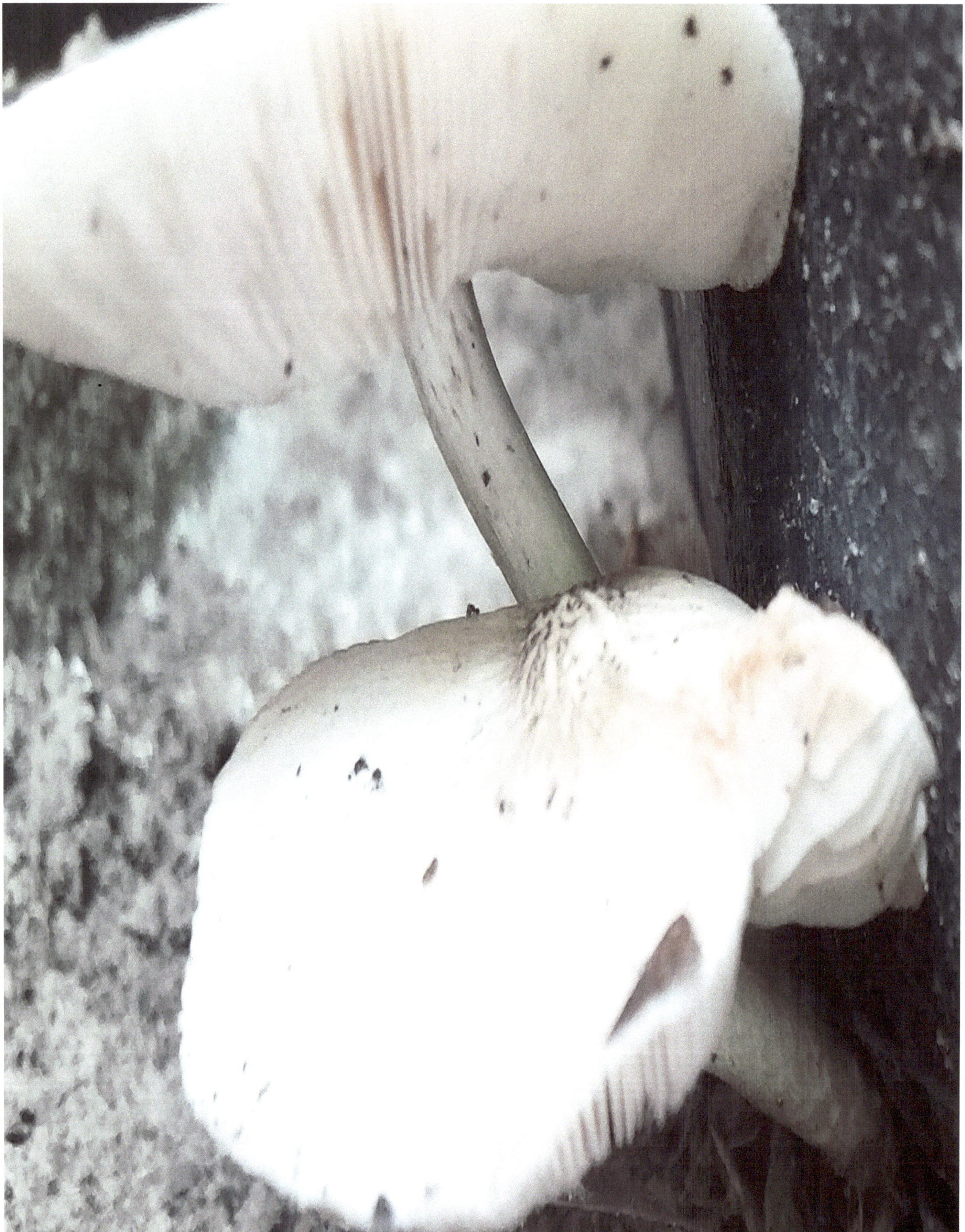

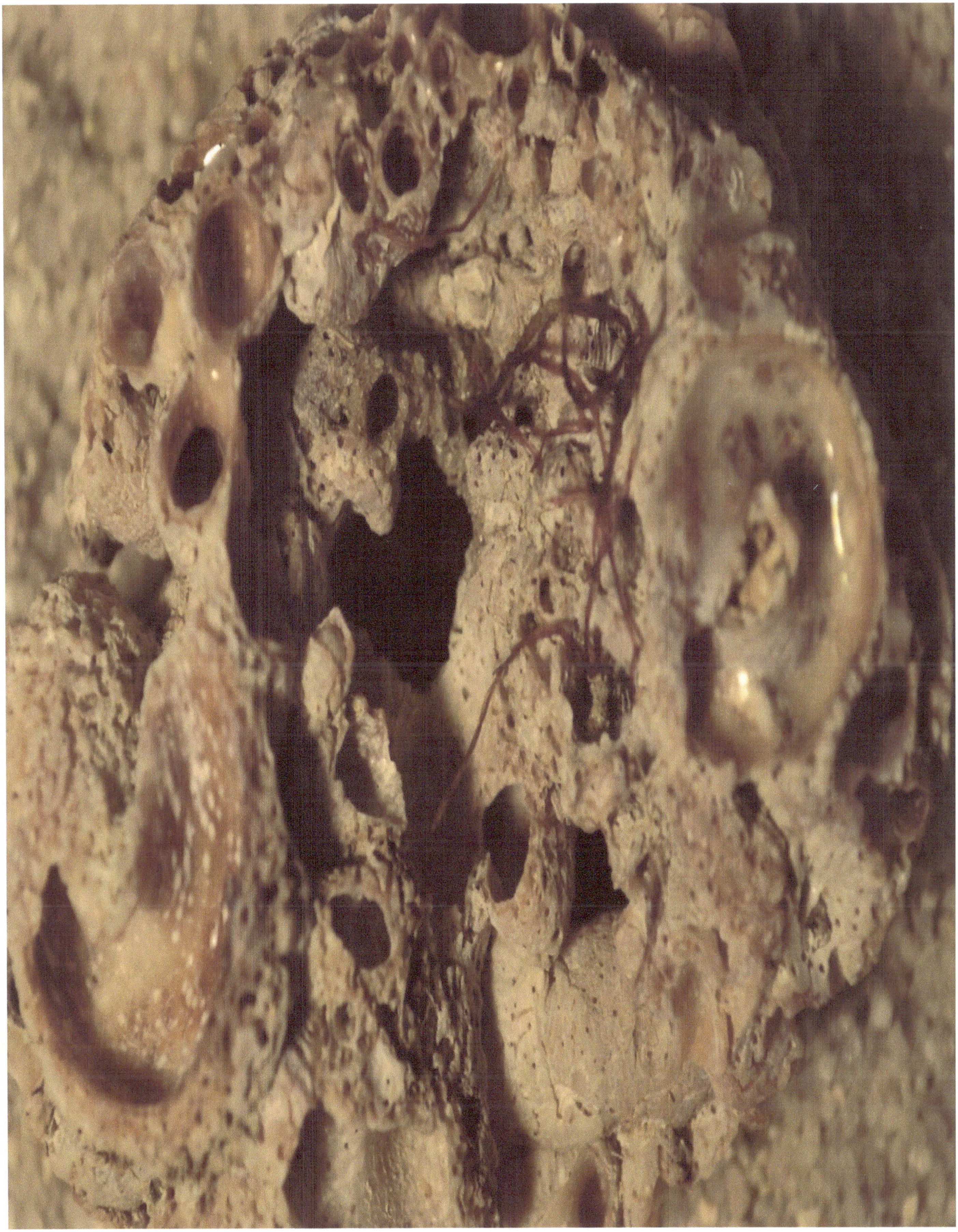

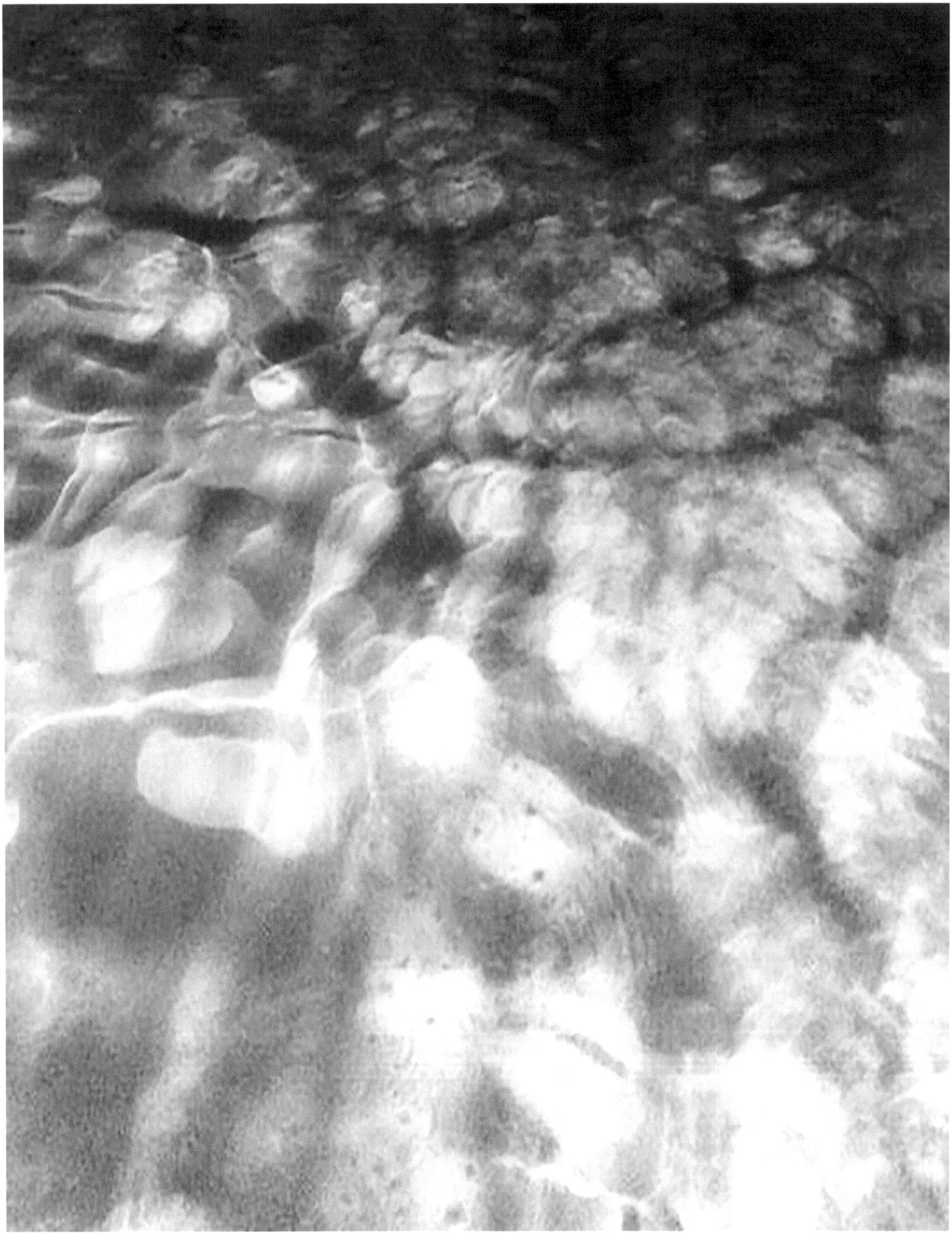

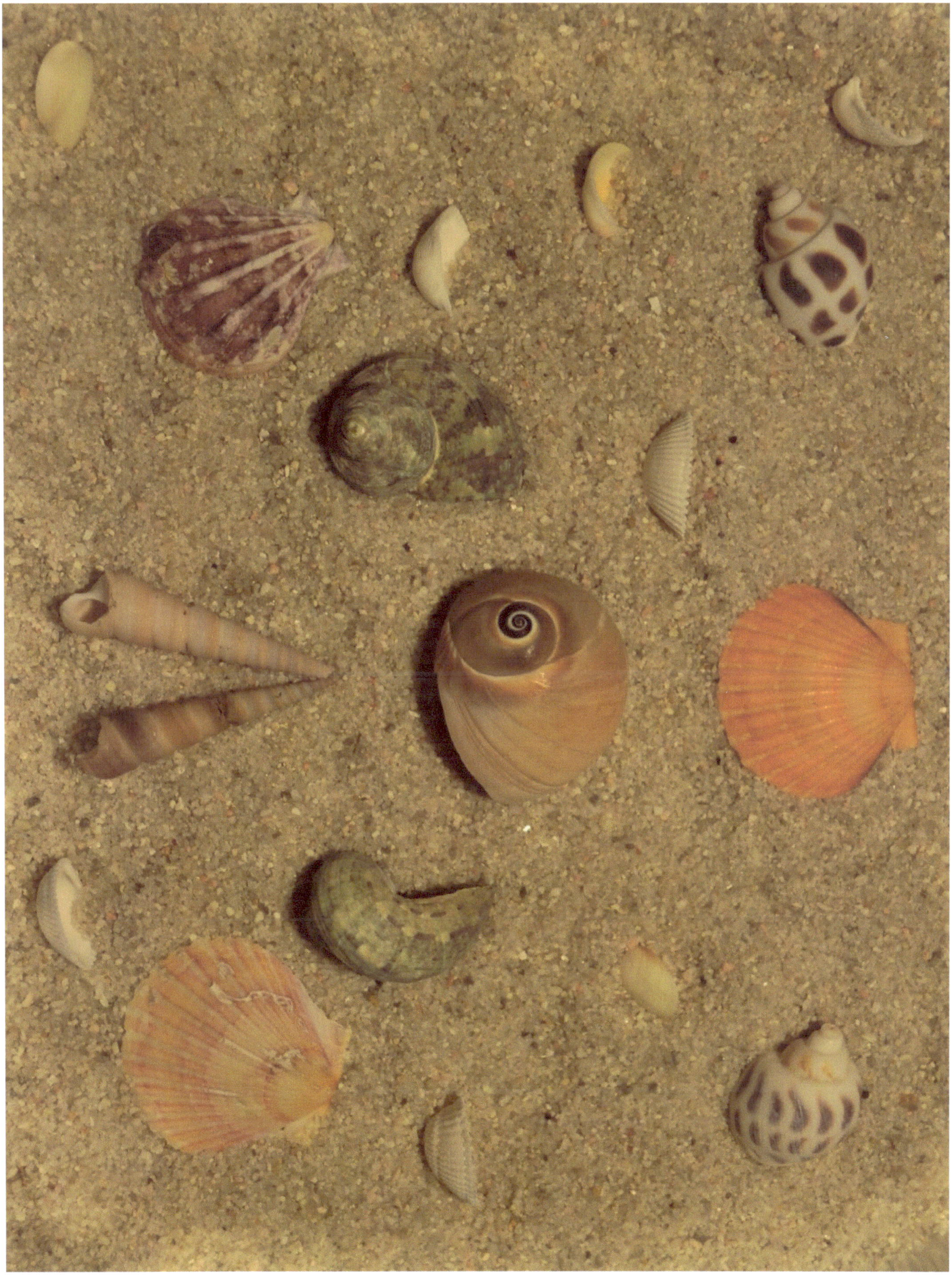

Thank God for all the blessings and gifts in my life!